BECOME A YOUTUBER — BUILD YOUR OWN YOUTUBE® CHANNEL

WILEY

BECOME A YOUTUBER — BUILD YOUR OWN YOUTUBE® CHANNEL

by Cristina Calabrese
The Digital Arts Experience

WILEY

BECOME A YOUTUBER — BUILD YOUR OWN YOUTUBE® CHANNEL

Published by: **John Wiley & Sons, Inc.**, 111 River Street, Hoboken, NJ 07030-5774, www.wiley.com

Copyright © 2018 by John Wiley & Sons, Inc., Hoboken, New Jersey

Published simultaneously in Canada

For general information on our other products and services, please contact our Customer Care Department within the U.S. at 877-762-2974, outside the U.S. at 317-572-3993, or fax 317-572-4002. For technical support, please visit https://hub.wiley.com/community/support/dummies.

Wiley publishes in a variety of print and electronic formats and by print-on-demand. Some material included with standard print versions of this book may not be included in e-books or in print-on-demand. If this book refers to media such as a CD or DVD that is not included in the version you purchased, you may download this material at http://booksupport.wiley.com. For more information about Wiley products, visit www.wiley.com.

Library of Congress Control Number: 2017959449

ISBN 978-1-119-40420-0 (pbk); ISBN 978-1-119-40428-6 (ePub); 978-1-119-40427-9 (ePDF)

Manufactured in the United States of America

10 9 8 7 6 5 4 3 2 1

CONTENTS AT A GLANCE

CONTENTS

CHAPTER

05 **Editing** 55

CHAPTER

06 **Uploading Your Video** 67

CHAPTER

07 Sharing Your Video

INTRODUCTION

So, you want to *Become a YouTuber,* but you're not sure where to begin. Or maybe you already have your own channel and are looking to step up your game and get more subscribers. Good news — building your own channel on YouTube may be easier than you think! It will take a lot of consistent work and dedication, but if the actual content that you're producing is something that is fun and you take pride in, your channel will grow naturally over time. The best part is that you are the owner, you are the content creator, and therefore you get to decide what is on your channel!

From video games and movie reviews to vlogging and funny reaction videos, there is an entire world out there on YouTube for you to not only explore, but join in on. This book focuses not so much on telling you what kind of content to create for your channel — that is totally up to you — but on how to build up your channel, create awesome videos, form a community, engage with your subscribers, earn money from advertisements, and grow to create your very own home on YouTube.

ABOUT THIS BOOK

YouTube was created in February 2005 and since then has grown to become one of the most frequented websites in the world. It has billions of active monthly users and is growing. Thanks to the popularity of YouTube, many tutorial and how-to videos are floating around the Internet. This book provides a complete introduction for you to get started on YouTube. I go in depth on how to make sure that your channel is properly set up, offer tips on creating good, consistent content, and, most importantly, explain how to engage your community to promote channel growth.

As time goes on, YouTube will change. Its basic purpose will always remain the same, but you may notice differences to the user interface. It's not uncommon for changes to the appearance and design to occur, so don't get overwhelmed if you log in one day, and things look different. This book has lots of screenshots and steps directing you how to complete certain tasks. There is a good chance that months and years from now, YouTube will look a little bit different, and that's fine. It's a living entity and constantly changing to improve itself. Try to focus on the end goal and what you're trying to accomplish. Sometimes the road to get somewhere changes, but reaching the end point is what matters.

Like content in all of the *For Dummies* series, this book will present its information in a fun, clear, and concise manner that I hope you enjoy.

FOOLISH ASSUMPTIONS

You may be new to YouTube, or you may be an avid YouTuber who uses it on a daily basis. Many people get into YouTubing with the prospect of becoming rich and famous. To set the record straight right away, it's very difficult to do that. It is entirely possible, but will take lots of consistent hard work and dedication to your channel. Don't foolishly assume that it's easy to become wealthy through YouTubing.

Sure, there is a chance that your video can go viral, and you can have overnight success. But in our society, today's viral video will be forgotten about by the end of the week. Nowadays, it is as if many, many videos go viral on a daily basis, but then fizzle out just as quickly.

The YouTube audience nowadays is extremely demanding. You need to release content on a regular basis, or you will be forgotten. That being said, YouTube audiences want to be entertained. They want to laugh. They want to learn something. Your goal is to attract their attention and get them hooked so that they will want to subscribe to your channel and come back for more.

In addition to that, I want you to keep an open mind when going through this book. You may think you already know everything about YouTube, and you could very well know a lot. But, you may be surprised to explore sections of this book discussing parts of YouTube that you were previously unaware of.

ICONS USED IN THIS BOOK

Throughout the margin of this book are little pictures known as icons. These icons have different meanings:

The Tip icon points out a tidbit of useful information.

This icon highlights something worth pointing out for you to keep in the back of your mind or even take note of.

WHERE TO GO FROM HERE

Become a YouTuber is divided into nine chapters, with each chapter focusing on different steps to help you create an exciting, entertaining, and successful YouTube channel. You do not need to read each of the chapters in order and can browse between them at your leisure. I want you to absorb the information in a way that is best for you! There is no correct way to learn, so take as much time as you need when you go through each chapter.

Whether you're new to YouTube, a casual user, or even an avid lover of binge-watching videos, this book aims to cater to a wide range of audiences. The beauty of not having to read the chapters in this book in order makes it easier for readers with varying skill levels to find content valuable to their needs.

If you're new to YouTube, you may want to consider starting with Chapter 1, which focuses mostly on the idea behind what makes a good channel, to set you up for success. The following chapters go through various tasks and goals from creating your channel's artwork all the way to studying analytics on how to improve. Feel free to skip around between the chapters to suit your needs.

01

Creating Awesome Content

So you want to become a YouTuber and build your own channel. Awesome! In this chapter, you discover the secrets to success, including connecting with your viewers and consistency.

THE THREE C'S OF YOUTUBE

When I take a step back and think about YouTube, I can divide it into three parts: Channel. Content. Community.

- Your **Channel** is your home base. When someone stumbles upon your channel, you want it to stand out. It's where you go to manage what viewers see. It is very important to have a channel theme and to stick to it. What do you want your channel to be about? Video Games? Music? Movies? It's up to you to decide. But once you do, make sure your channel is dedicated to that and only that! In this book, I help you get your channel up and running.

- **Content** is the heart of your channel — the blood that flows through its veins. Without content, your channel is just an empty shell. YouTube is driven by content. Coming up with creative, unique content and uploading consistently can be very challenging. In this book, I cover the best practices for producing awesome content in a fun and easy way.

- **Community** is the third part of YouTube and also extremely unpredictable. Community mostly consists of your audience but includes other YouTubers as well. You can't predict how the community will react to your videos. But, by being an active member and studying the performance of your videos, you'll be able to adapt and make changes to better the success of your own content. In this book, I explore ways you can interact with the community, track performance of your videos, and evolve in order to stay on top of your game.

RECOGNIZING THE IMPORTANCE OF COMMUNITY

YouTube is one of the most visited websites in the world, with billions of visitors each month. In this current age of new technologies developing faster than we can blink, YouTube itself has certainly evolved over the years. But what hasn't changed is that it has always been driven by user content. That means unique and entertaining videos from users like you!

With YouTube accessible in so many countries around the world, it has connected humans in a way that had never been done before.

The most important thing to keep in mind when building your own channel is that YouTube is more than just a place to share videos. What makes YouTube shine is its community.

Standing out on YouTube is a huge challenge, but the most successful YouTubers have found ways to grow their channels by connecting with their audiences.

YouTubers are able to upload any kind of video they want — within the terms of service, of course. With millions upon millions of videos, you can find virtually anything on YouTube, such as movie, TV show, and video game reviews, travel experiences, comedy, and tutorials — the possibilities are endless!

If you want to learn the Korean alphabet, try YouTube! Want to watch an 80-year-old blacksmith weld a knife with his bare hands? YouTube. How about reviews of your favorite video games? If you can imagine it, chances are, there is already a video of it somewhere on YouTube. The best part is the videos are accessible to the public, and anyone with a valid Gmail account can create their very own channel.

REMEMBER

How you interact with your community is what really drives your channel's success.

Quite simply, your community is way more than just your audience. It refers to the theme of your channel, your video content, your viewers, subscribers, and comments, and the ways your channel can cast a ripple in the vast ocean that is YouTube. These are all just fancy ways for me to tell you to stay active!

As with any community, being an active part of one means making contributions. With consistency and good content, you can easily become an active member of the YouTube community.

Ways to stay active include

- Uploading new content regularly

- Always responding to comments

- Visiting similar channels

- Engaging with people who have similar interests

You need to add value to your community by providing something unique and original. Thousands of YouTubers are out there — what makes the top channels stand out? And why would someone want to watch your videos?

COMING UP WITH A THEME

Before you even make your first video, you must come up with a theme for your channel.

If you want to be a YouTuber, chances are you already have a few ideas in mind. Whatever you choose — whether it's a gaming channel or a channel reviewing your favorite tech devices — make sure that you stick to that one topic.

Center your channel around something that you truly love doing or talking about. Otherwise, creating videos over time will just start to feel like a chore for you.

I'm going to assume that you already have a good idea for a channel theme. But just in case you don't, some of the most popular YouTube channels are

- Comedy

- Education & Tutorials

- Gaming

- Music

- Pet Videos

- Reactions

- Unboxing New Products

- Vlogging

Is there a channel theme not listed here that you are a fan of? Don't be afraid to come up with something original. If you have an idea for a new channel, ask a few friends what they think. Their opinion could really help you form your channel's identity. Would your friends watch your videos? If not, why would a user on YouTube be compelled to watch?

One thing I want to point out, which should go without saying, is if you ever involve an animal or pet in one of your videos, please make sure that you are safe and do not harm them.

CONSISTENCY IS KEY

Character, personality, and consistency will keep your audience coming back for more. You'll want to make an impression and leave an impact so that viewers will want to subscribe to your channel! *Consistency* not only means uploading new videos on a regular basis, but also the way in which your videos are created.

Take a look at three videos from one of your favorite top YouTubers. You'll notice that each video has a similar format. Usually they start with an intro, get into the main portion, and then an outro.

So in essence, they

- Tell you what the video will be about

- Show you what the video will be about

- Recap and invite you to return (by subscribing)

When planning your videos, keep their format similar. Your viewers will begin to expect a certain layout for each video, and drastically changing things up can deter people from coming back.

Here are some things to think about:

- What category would your YouTube channel fall under?

- Who would be watching your videos?

- Why would someone watch your videos?

- Is this topic something you won't get sick of over time?

- Will you easily be able to create new content on a regular basis?

- How often do you want to upload?

THE SUCCESS FORMULA

There is no exact formula that will guarantee success. YouTubers are always looking for new, creative ways to stay relevant with different strategies. If there was a blueprint to follow, this book would sure be a lot different! Success comes in many forms and you can begin to gauge your success by keeping track of milestones.

A milestone is an event that marks an achievement. Channel milestones can include reaching a certain number of subscribers, channel views, and uploaded videos, to name a few.

What are some milestones that you hope to achieve on your channel?

By following a few of these best practices for YouTube, you will put your-self in the best position to gain traction:

- **Create an upload schedule.**   Figure out which days of the week you'll release new videos. I would recommend starting simple like once a week, and as you get a better feel for things, up it to twice a week and go from there.

- **Upload consistently.** After you have a schedule set, be sure to upload consistently. This consistency will keep your audience happy, and show that your channel is alive.

- **Change is good.** Be open to changing things up. If you notice after a month that all of your videos have under ten views, clearly something isn't working. Try using different titles, descriptions, thumbnails, tags, and so on.

- **Just stay active.** Stumbling on a channel where the last video was uploaded two months ago does not look like a very active channel. YouTubers are actively creating content on a regular basis, and people are more likely to subscribe to a channel that has an active appearance.

GOING VIRAL

I'm going to be completely honest with you. Most videos go viral by accident. The formula for creating a viral video is a mystery that no one can exactly figure out. In case you're unfamiliar with what *going viral* refers to, it is simply a video that gets insanely popular in a short amount of time. And by popular, I'm talking millions of views within a few days.

Some YouTubers have gotten famous off of viral videos, but it is completely by chance. Having a video go viral is as unpredictable as guessing winning lottery numbers. No one has been able to come up with an exact formula behind the science of a viral video. For whatever reason, users feel compelled to share it. Have you ever taken a look at a viral video and wondered why it became so popular?

Think about some of your favorite videos on YouTube. Why are they popular? Here are a few possible reasons:

- **They're funny.** How often do you find yourself watching a funny video on YouTube that you want to share with someone? I bet it's happened pretty often! A lot of these videos aren't traditionally funny, but there's something about them that's original and uniquely humorous. Users love watching content that makes them laugh.

- **They're random.** The video "Charlie Bit Me!" comes to mind as an example of a completely random, yet charming, video in that something was caught completely in a single moment of time that won't ever happen again. Many viral videos are chance moments that have happened to have been caught on camera. If you haven't seen that video, check it out!

- **They got shared a lot.**   The main reason a video goes viral is that it gets shared over and over again. If the right person watches it and shares, it could have incredible reach. Think of a celebrity with millions of followers sharing your video. Each one of their followers then has the potential to also share your video to their followers. The possibilities are endless, and the reason why videos go viral so quickly. Think about strategic platforms you can share your videos on.

If for some reason you get lucky with a viral video, without having the practices described in this chapter in place, a viral video could just be 15 minutes of fame and nothing more. By creating a consistent routine and building a solid foundation on your channel, you can set yourself up for success without needing a viral video to propel you to stardom.

THE SIX-MONTH CHALLENGE

REMEMBER

You're not going to be an overnight success. These things take lots of hard work, dedication, and consistency. Know your strengths by finding out what you're good at. Some YouTubers can create absolutely hilarious 10-minute video compilations of cats and dogs. Others are really talented gamers who are exciting to watch. Some are really informative at reviewing products. What's your purpose going to be?

When I decided that I wanted to grow my own YouTube channel with only 27 subscribers, I challenged myself to get 1,000 subscribers in six months. At almost six months exactly to the date, I had organically hit 1,000 subscribers and received my first payment from YouTube ad revenue.

Growing my channel wasn't easy, and many times, I neglected my channel, asking myself "What's the point?" But, something always brought me back. Once I realized that creating content on YouTube was something I was really passionate about, the whole process suddenly stopped feeling like work. Instead, I started to enjoy the entire process — from coming up with an idea, filming, editing, uploading, and then studying the analytics over time.

SHORT-TERM VERSUS LONG-TERM GOALS

You can accomplish a short-term goal within a few days or weeks, whereas a long-term goal can span months or even years. What are some short-term goals you've accomplished in your life in the past? How about long-term?

Examples of short-term goals include

- Upload a new video once a week

- Log in daily to check for comments

- Check a video's analytics after one week

Here are a few examples of long-term goals:

- Get 1,000 subscribers in six months

- Get 100,000 views in six months

- Create a website for your brand

CREATING YOUR OWN GOALS

Think about your own goals that you want to set for your channel. How many are short term? What about long term? Don't be afraid to write them down and assign due dates. What can be accomplished in the short term? What is a work in progress that you can accomplish over a longer period of time?

Set some goals that you can accomplish once a week. Now set a six-month challenge goal for yourself. What do you envision your channel to look like six months from now? Hold yourself accountable.

REMEMBER

YouTube is constantly changing, and every second, millions of users are generating new content. As a YouTuber, you are part of this phenomenon. This means you need to constantly find ways to stay relevant. A huge part of being a YouTuber is to also remain a viewer. Watch other channels often. Be aware of what's trending. Always ask yourself "How can I do better?"

CHAPTER

02

Setting Up Your Channel

A huge part of becoming a YouTuber has to do with how your channel appears to people who stumble upon it. You want it to look clean and uniform. Your channel icon, banner, and name should all have a similar theme. This advice also applies to how you release your content.

In this chapter, I explore how you can set the tone on your channel for a new viewer.

SETTING UP YOUR ACCOUNT

You may already have a YouTube account, but if you don't, creating a new account is pretty simple:

1. **Head on over to YouTube.com from your preferred web browser.**

2. **Click on Sign In in the upper-right corner (see Figure 2-1).**

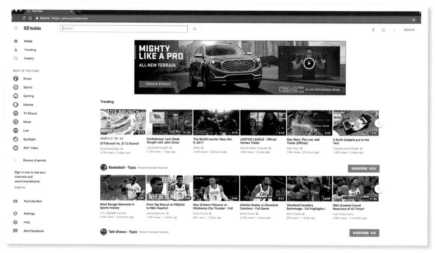

Figure 2-1: Click on Sign In to create an account.

3. **In the next screen that appears, click on More options (see Figure 2-2).**

4. **Click on Create Account, as shown in Figure 2-3.**

Figure 2-2: Click on More options to see additional choices.

5. **Create your Google Account by following the on-screen instructions, as shown in Figure 2-4.**

   Great! Now you're all set!

Figure 2-3: Click on the option to create a new account.

Head on back to YouTube.com, and you should be logged into your account. If you aren't, click Sign In and log in with your Google account and password.

Figure 2-4: Fill out the form to create your own Google Account.

NAVIGATING YOUR CHANNEL

If you're comfortable with the user interface, you can easily navigate around YouTube. For this section, I'm going to assume you are still logged in and are somewhere — it could be anywhere — on the YouTube website.

To navigate your channel:

1. **Click on your user icon in the top-right corner of your screen.**

    Your default icon will look different from mine, which is pictured in Figure 2-5. The user icon is always visible no matter where you are on YouTube (see Figure 2-6).

    After you click on your user icon, a menu appears, offering several options (see Figure 2-7), including

    - **My channel:** See an overview of your channel.

    - **Creator Studio:** A major hub for all things related to managing your channel, community, analytics, and more.

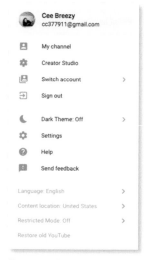

Figure 2-5: Click the user icon in the top-right corner of YouTube.

Figure 2-6: Your user icon appears throughout YouTube.

- **Switch Account:** If you have multiple YouTube accounts, you can easily switch between them.

- **Sign out:** Self-explanatory — always remember to sign out if you aren't on your own personal computer.

- **Dark Theme:** Can be On or Off, based on your visual preference. You can switch between Dark and Light Theme to change the colors on your YouTube screen.

- **Settings:** How you access your account settings.

- **Help:** Search for any questions you may have.

- **Send Feedback:** Give suggestions to YouTube.

2. **Click on My Channel.**

    You see your channel. You can see an example in Figure 2-8. See whether you can identify your

    - Channel Banner

    - User Icon

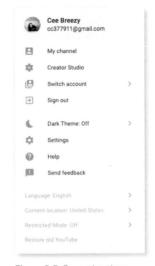

Figure 2-7: Several options appear when you click on your user icon once logged into YouTube. My Channel will take you to your main channel view.

Figure 2-8: What a YouTube channel looks like when the owner of the channel is logged in and viewing it.

REMEMBER

If you've just created a new account, chances are you'll have a default channel icon and banner. Also, the way videos are arranged on your channel overview may look different from those pictured in Figure 2-8 — especially if you haven't uploaded your first video yet.

- Channel Name

- Number of subscribers

- Customize Channel button

- Creator Studio button

CUSTOMIZING YOUR ACCOUNT SETTINGS

Under your Account Settings, you can customize a few of your channel features, such as your channel's name, connections to social media accounts, and more.

TIP

I recommend customizing your account settings after creating a new account just so that you can get some of the one-time setup tasks out of the way.

COMING UP WITH A GOOD NAME

One of the first things you want to consider is what your channel name will be. Your channel name is going to be a huge part of your identity on YouTube, so you really want to come up with something original and creative.

TIP

Consider your name creation. Have you asked yourself what's in a good name? Not only do you want a name you like, but it should be memorable. You want it to relate to your channel's theme.

Got a gaming channel? Why not something straight to the point, such as *Your_Name* Gaming. Without even watching a video, a viewer will instantly be able to know what your channel is about.

Try to write down a few words that describe your personality and your channel. Are there any clever words you can combine together?

When naming your channel, avoid

- Long names

- Names with lots of numbers

- Alternating caps

- Lots of special characters ($, !, %, and so on)

After you decide on a name, ask yourself:

- Does it clearly define my channel's theme?

- Is it family-friendly?

- Is it a name I can associate with on a long-term basis?

 REMEMBER

Just imagine your channel really blows up. What if you're stuck with a name that you don't like? Take some serious thought before you set your channel name.

While creating a name you like is important and I do encourage you to come up with a name related to your channel's theme, sometimes the most popular YouTube channels have the strangest names! If you already have a fun name that you think people will remember, don't be afraid to go for it. In the end, you need to be happy with it.

SETTING YOUR CHANNEL NAME

You can set your channel name in your account settings. To do so, make sure that you're still logged in to your YouTube account and follow these steps:

1. **Click on your user icon in the top right corner of your screen.**

2. **Click on Settings, as shown in Figure 2-9.**

   From Settings, you'll be able to edit your channel name directly.

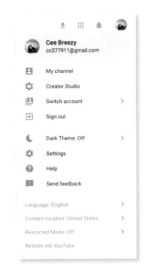

Figure 2-9: Click on Settings to access your entire channel's Account Settings.

3. **Click on Edit on Google, as shown in Figure 2-10.**

Figure 2-10: Click on Edit on Google to change your channel name.

4. **Type your First and Last Name, Nickname, and Display Name as shown in Figure 2-11.**

   Your Display Name is what users will see as your name when they visit your channel or view your videos.

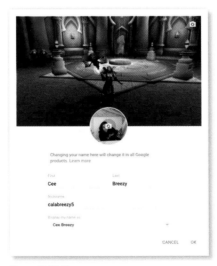

Figure 2-11: Set your name.

5. **After you're happy with your name, click on OK to set it.**

Be careful! After you set your name, you may not be able to change it.

Your name may take anywhere from a few minutes to a few hours to update on your channel, so if it doesn't update right away, don't worry!

CONNECTING YOUR SOCIAL MEDIA ACCOUNTS

In Account settings, you can connect your Twitter account to your YouTube channel, as well as alter how you'd like to share your activity:

1. **In the Settings screen, click on your user icon.**

2. **Click on Settings.**

3. **Click on Connected accounts.**

   The Connected accounts screen appears, as shown in Figure 2-12.

Figure 2-12: The Connected accounts screen.

4. **Link Twitter by clicking on the Connect button next to the Twitter icon (see Figure 2-13).**

Figure 2-13: The Connect button.

5. **Choose your preference by clicking on the appropriate checkbox under Share your public activity to connected accounts (see Figure 2-14).**

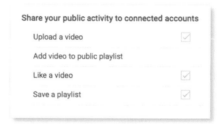

Figure 2-14: You can choose how you'd like to share your public activity on your social media accounts.

By checking one of these boxes after connecting your Twitter account, you'll automatically send a tweet when you

- Upload a video

- Add video to a public playlist

- Like a video

- Save a playlist

6. **Once you're happy with your selections, click on Save.**

SETTING PRIVACY AND NOTIFICATIONS

The Account settings offer additional options for you to go through in order to further customize your channel. In the Privacy screen, shown in Figure 2-15, you can choose whether you want your own Likes and Subscriptions to be public or private.

Figure 2-15: The Privacy screen.

Under Activity Feed, shown in Figure 2-16, you can decide whether you want these options to be public or private. Go through the settings and customize them how you like. Don't forget to save before advancing.

In Notification settings, shown in Figure 2-17, you can further customize when you want to be notified via email of certain actions on YouTube. If you notice you get too many emails and want to reduce the number, this screen is the place to be. Go through each section and select or deselect accordingly.

REMEMBER

Whenever you add a video to a playlist, like a video, subscribe to a channel, and more, you can choose to have this activity posted on your channel.

Activity Feed

Decide if you want to post your public actions to your activity feed. Your actions on private videos will not be posted. Your posts to your feed may also show up on connected apps or websites.

Post to my activity feed when I...

☑ Add video to public playlist

☑ Like a video ⓘ

☑ Save a playlist ⓘ

☑ Subscribe to a channel ⓘ

Save

Figure 2-16: You can customize your activity feed to decide what is public and what is private.

Figure 2-17: The Notification settings allow you to change how you want to be notified via email of certain events on YouTube.

CHOOSING A GOOD CHANNEL ICON

After combing through a bunch of your account settings, you can now move on to more creative tasks, such as choosing a channel icon. A good channel icon can attract viewers to your channel. Sometimes referred to as a *profile picture,* your channel icon is featured prominently under all your videos next to your username.

You'll want an icon that represents your channel or personality. It can be a simple picture of you from a webcam, or it can be a screenshot from one of your videos. Either way, be sure it does not contain anything inappropriate or something that may break the YouTube rules and user agreement.

File format must be JPG, GIF, BMP, or a PNG file. 800 x 800 pixels is the recommended size. Ensure that the image is either square or round.

After you find a good picture, you can upload it to your account. To change your channel icon:

1. **Click on your user icon in the top-right corner of your screen.**

2. **Click on My Channel.**

   Your Channel Overview page appears.

3. **Click on the blue Customize Channel button (see Figure 2-18).**

Figure 2-18: The Customize Channel button allows you to make creative changes to your channel.

4. **Hover over the default icon in the upper-left corner of your banner.**

   A pencil, shown in Figure 2-19, appears.

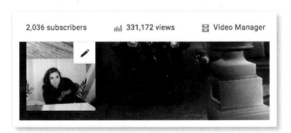

Figure 2-19: After you hover over the icon, a pencil appears, allowing you to click on it to change your icon.

5. **Click on the pencil to edit your channel icon.**

   The Edit channel icon dialog box, shown in Figure 2-20, pops up to tell you that it may take a few minutes for your updated icon to appear.

6. **Click on Edit.**

Edit channel icon

Your channel icon comes from your Google account. Changes may take a few minutes to show on your channel.

CANCEL   EDIT

Figure 2-20: Google warns you that it may take a little bit of time to see the new icon update.

7. **Upload your image from your computer.**

8. **Click on Done once you're happy with your choice.**

   After you set an icon, your channel starts to come together.

I strongly recommend you upload your own channel icon as soon as you can. Using the default YouTube icon isn't really a good look for your channel. It could give users the false impression that your channel isn't active or not taken very seriously.

REMEMBER

A nice, uniform-looking channel will hold a viewer's interest much more than a sloppy one. If you want to win over viewers to transform them into subscribers, prove to them that you take your channel seriously. By having a nice channel name, icon, and banner, it shows you put effort into your channel.

Additionally, after you set your name, icon, and banner, chances are you'll keep them for a good while. Taking the time to create quality artwork will pay off in long-term results.

CREATING A CHANNEL BANNER

Your banner shows prominently on your channel's main page. You definitely want something attractive that portrays your channel's identity in some way. Do you have a gaming channel? Why not add in a picture of a video game controller?

Make sure that your channel banner is unique and related to your channel's theme.

Bannersnack is a great website (www.bannersnack.com) and is free to sign up. It allows you to make free banners with predesigned templates. Alternatively, Canva (www.canva.com/create/banners/youtube-banners) is a great all-around graphic design website that allows you to make a plethora of images, including thumbnails for your YouTube videos. It's free to sign up and also very easy to use.

Want to custom design your own in Photoshop or another program? Use the custom dimensions 2560 x 1440 pixels and make sure it's under 6MB to do it yourself!

To upload a channel banner:

1. **Click on your user icon in the top-right corner of your screen.**

2. **Click on My Channel.**
   You see your Channel Overview page.

3. **Click on the blue Customize Channel button.**

4. **Hover over the default icon in the upper-left corner of your banner.**
   A pencil appears.

5. **Click on the pencil to edit your channel banner.**

6. **Click on Edit channel art, as shown in Figure 2-21.**

7. **Upload your desired image.**

Figure 2-21: Click on the pencil.

ADDING SOCIAL ICONS TO YOUR BANNER

Under your channel banner on the right side is a space to add social media icons. Here, you can add in a website if you have one, Twitter, Facebook, Instagram, and other links that your viewers may also be interested in checking out.

To customize what you'd like featured:

1. **Click on your user icon in the top-right corner of your screen.**

2. **Click on My Channel.**

   Your Channel Overview page appears.

3. **Click on the blue Customize Channel button.**

4. **Click on About, shown in Figure 2-22.**

Figure 2-22: Click on About to customize your channel's social media links.

5. **Hover over each section and click on the pencil icon to edit a particular section.**

You can edit your channel description on this page, too! Describe the theme of your channel in just a few sentences. Tell users why they should subscribe to your channel. You can also include how often you'll update videos or little facts about yourself that are interesting.

GETTING STARTED WITH GRAPHIC DESIGN

Graphic design simply refers to the skill of creating visual artwork with images, text, and other assets. Back in the day, many people would study for years to become proficient at graphic design. Fortunately, with today's technology and a few key pointers, even a beginner can create some really cool artwork!

Here are a few tips to help you out with graphic design, especially if you're completely new to it:

- **Use consistent font faces.** If your design has a lot of text, a good general rule is to use no more than two or three different font faces. Using too many different kinds of fonts is overwhelming and will distract the viewer from the actual message.

- **Make your text easy to read.** Try to limit the amount of wording you use. Think about when you write a long Twitter message and then have to make it shorter so that it fits in your tweet. Keep brevity in mind when designing graphics.

- **Less is more.** Don't try to overwhelm your viewers. Make sure that you know what you're trying to portray and think about the simplest way to do so. After you finish an initial mockup, take a look and think of ways you can simplify it.

- **Pay attention to scale.** There's nothing more unprofessional than an image that isn't scaled proportionally. Remember to always keep the aspect ratio intact. In most programs, holding down Shift while you drag to adjust the size of an image will keep the scale proportioned.

FIGURING OUT WHAT PROGRAMS TO USE

Many people use Photoshop for graphic design. Although it requires a paid subscription to use, you can sign up for a free trial at www.adobe. com/photoshop. This way, you can get a feel for the program before you decide whether it's something you'd like to purchase.

Pixlr is a great free alternative to Photoshop. What's great is that it's web-based so that you can work on it from any computer, save your progress on your account, and resume working whenever you feel like it. To find out more about Pixlr, check out its website to make a free account: www.pixlr.com.

Canva (www.canva.com) is another super-easy, popular graphic design platform that is free and web-based. Not only can you use Canva to make a channel banner, but you can easily create an account and use one of its many templates to create designs ranging from YouTube channel art, Facebook cover photo, email header and more! Canva has a drag-and-drop interface and is really easy to use, especially if you have no prior graphic design experience!

CHAPTER

03

Creating an Intro Trailer

After you have a good idea of what type of content you'll be producing, it's time to get busy! In this chapter, you discover how to create an intro trailer so that new viewers can learn about your channel. Your trailer is going to be very similar to a movie trailer. It's a great way to preview your content with the goal to get viewers to subscribe.

Have you ever sat through all those previews before seeing a movie? How often has one of those previews compelled you to then go see that movie? Think about why your channel is unique and why a viewer would want to subscribe. Let your personality shine brightly!

In Chapter 4, I cover shooting video in more detail, but in this chapter, I make the process of creating your trailer straightforward and simple.

BREAKING DOWN THE PROCESS

In creating this trailer, you use a process that you can apply to any video. You can break down this process into a few steps:

1. **Brainstorm.**

2. **Film and edit.**

3. **Upload.**

With these key concepts, you can set yourself up for success. It may seem very simple, but you should take each part of the process seriously to product quality content.

BRAINSTORMING

The process of creating a trailer starts with the brainstorm. Your channel trailer is a great way to turn viewers into subscribers. You'll need to capture their attention quickly and cover your channel's theme in a fun and unique way. Try your best to give the viewers a reason to want to subscribe!

Here are a few channel trailer quick tips:

- **Grab their attention within the first few seconds.**

- **Keep it short — under 1 minute.**

- **Assume the viewer has never been to your channel before.**

- **Ask your viewers to subscribe at the end.**

FIGURING OUT WHAT YOU'LL COVER

So, what will you cover in your trailer? Give an overview of your channel, such as what your channel is about and what viewers can expect in your videos. But also let your personality shine through.

After you establish something exciting and unique about your channel within the first few seconds of your trailer, in a few sentences or less, make sure that the viewer properly understands the theme of your channel. Explain your channel's purpose in a clear and concise way.

REMEMBER

You want to hook the viewer in right away. Be sure to have the most important information about your channel in the beginning. If there's something really exciting about your channel, share it right away! This is a great method to hook a viewer and encourage them to keep watching.

Gather some ideas to brainstorm by writing things down. Even if you just start with a bunch of random words, it's a great way to get ideas down on paper. Words can be expanded into thoughts, and those thoughts can be expanded into sentences.

THINKING ABOUT PROPS

Don't forget to think about any props, settings, or costumes that you may need. Can you film it all in front of your computer, or do you need another area?

Sets, props, and costumes can all add emphasis to a scene. Chances are you're just starting out with a new channel, so I recommend starting simple, especially if you don't have much of a budget.

Can you create any props or costumes yourself? Why not use your resources and check YouTube for DIY (do-it-yourself) prop and costume ideas?

Get all your ideas written down together in one spot, even if they seem really crazy at the time.

The following sections describe a few examples of channel trailers.

DAILY BUMPS

Daily Bumps (see Figure 3-1) is a family-focused channel that creates videos about everyday life activates featuring two parents and their kids. From getting haircuts to eating challenges, this channel can turn a boring everyday task into something exciting. You can view their channel trailer at www.youtube.com/watch?v=Z2KhIndJSTY.

Figure 3-1: A channel trailer from Daily Bumps.

Their trailer catches your attention right away with quick shots of a T-Rex costume, a gorilla suit, underwater shots, and more of the family. The music sounds cinematic just like a movie trailer, and the added-in sound effects add to the viewer experience. Their trailer does a great job allowing the viewer to learn some things about their channel all while creating a fun and exciting trailer.

STAMPY

Stampy (see Figure 3-2) is a gaming personality on YouTube who mostly specializes in Minecraft. His channel trailer is a few years old, but offers an alternative way you can create one for new viewers: www.youtube.com/watch?v=KOFm-JBOqFc.

Stampy starts off right away with an introduction: who he is, what he does, and how often he uploads videos. An introduction is a great way to hook in a new viewer by sharing details about your channel in a quick and concise way. Stampy then proceeds to highlight a bunch of his best clips of gameplay, mostly in Minecraft.

Figure 3-2: Stampy's channel trailer.

JENERATIONDIY

JENerationDIY (see Figure 3-3) is a channel by a girl named Jen with videos on DIY (do-it-yourself), fashion, beauty, food, and comedy skits: www.youtube.com/watch?v=9gxcqzKCFSU.

Figure 3-3: JENerationDIY's channel trailer.

Jen's intro trailer starts with vibey, upbeat music, quick cuts, and a general introduction. She discusses what her channel is about and gives you a glimpse into her life. Instead of a lot of talking, she allows the viewers to see for themselves by showing lots of fast cuts from her videos. It's quick, but just enough to hook viewers in so that they want to learn more.

Take a look at your favorite YouTubers' trailers and see what they've done that makes you interested in their content. Don't be afraid to get inspiration from other channels. There's no harm in getting ideas from a few different channels and then forming your own.

CHOOSING MUSIC

Think about any music that you want to add in to supplement the trailer. Music can really help set your tone. Is your channel fun and exciting? Look for music that will reflect that mood.

In the case of a channel trailer, you want to hook viewers in within the first few seconds. Therefore, try to find music that is exciting and upbeat!

YouTube has its own Audio Library (www.youtube.com/audiolibrary/music), shown in Figure 3-4, with all royalty-free music that you can download.

In the Audio Library, you can select length, genre, mood, and much more.

Figure 3-4: YouTube's royalty-free Audio Library with songs you can download to use for your videos.

WRITING A SCRIPT

Writing a script is recommended so that when you film your video, you already know ahead of time what you're going to say. Writing a script will save you lots of time.

Some people have the ability to ad-lib or just speak freely. If you are confident in your ability to do that, by all means give it a shot. But writing down your thoughts and direction for the video will really provide structure and make the whole production process easier. With a script, you can take your time recording the video. Whether you memorize it or not, you can film it all in one take. Or, you can recite a few lines at a time with breaks in the middle.

STORYBOARDING

A *storyboard* is a visual way to lay out plans for a shooting a video. Storyboarding is accomplished by using graphics and drawings with something as simple as a piece of paper and pencil. It can help with different scenes, shots, angles and general flow. Storyboards help you visualize a basic way your video will run from start to finish.

Figure 3-5 explains what a storyboard is and how to utilize it.

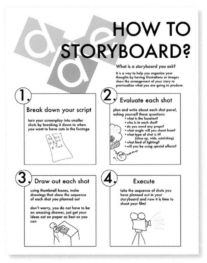

Figure 3-5: A storyboard helps you plan your video.

If you'd prefer the traditional hand-drawn method of storyboarding, search online for 'free storyboard paper' that you can print out to use to help visualize your script.

Storyboard That is a great online storyboard creation tool. You can create scenes and storylines all digitally. Check it out for free at www.storyboardthat.com.

REMEMBER

You don't have to be an amazing artist to utilize storyboard paper. Stick figures work out fine as long as they help demonstrate each scene!

Most storyboard papers have several boxes per page where you can doodle shot ideas, with some space underneath for notes.

Try to storyboard your video ideas. You may be surprised to find that it will really help you organize your thoughts. A lot of times, I really prefer writing ideas down before I even do any work on the computer.

FILMING AND UPLOADING YOUR TRAILER

After you figure out what you're going to say, you need tools to record your trailer. Most YouTubers use either webcams, smartphones, or a digital camera. (Refer to Chapter 4 for a more detailed breakdown of cameras and shot types).

Whichever method you decide to use, just remember to try and keep it simple. If you are new to filming, start basic and expand over time. Find out what type of workflow works best for you.

> **TIP**
>
> I recommend shooting a single video under 20 seconds for your first channel trailer with a basic webcam. Remember to keep your channel trailer short and to the point. Grab the viewer's attention immediately and win them over by talking about why your channel is awesome!

To upload your trailer, make sure that you're logged in to your YouTube account and follow these steps:

1. **Click on the Upload icon, shown in Figure 3-6.**

   It looks like an arrow facing up.

2. **On the next screen, upload your trailer (see Figure 3-7).**

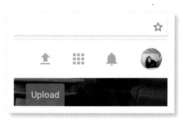

Figure 3-6: By clicking on the upward facing arrow, you can upload your channel trailer.

Figure 3-7: Upload a video.

You can save a few clicks by directly going to www.youtube.com/upload. Just make sure that you're logged in to your account.

SETTING YOUR CHANNEL TRAILER

After your trailer is all set and uploaded, think about setting a good title and description. The title can be anything simple, such as "My Channel Trailer." Add a few sentences under the video in the description field below.

If you'd like to go into detail with tilting, tagging, description, thumbnail, and all those other features you see when you upload a video, refer to Chapter 6. But for now, just adding a title and description is fine.

You also need to make sure that the trailer is featured on your landing page. Follow these steps:

1. **Click on your user icon in the top-right corner of your screen (see Figure 3-8).**

Figure 3-8: Your user icon is on the upper right-hand corner of YouTube.

2. **Click on My channel, as shown in Figure 3-9.**

   Your Channel Overview page appears.

3. **Click on the blue Customize Channel button, shown in Figure 3-10.**

4. **Hover your mouse over the area where you see a pencil icon shown in Figure 3-11.**

5. **When a pencil appears, click on it to edit.**

6. **Click on For new visitors, as shown in Figure 3-12.**

7. **Click on Change trailer, as shown in Figure 3-13.**

   A new window appears with any and all of your uploaded videos.

8. **Select whichever video your trailer is and then click on Save.**

After you set a trailer for your channel, whenever a new viewer stumbles upon your channel, your trailer will be visible for them to watch.

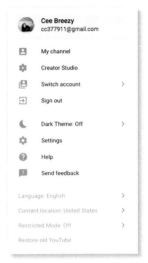

Figure 3-9: My channel is the first option that appears after clicking on your user icon.

Figure 3-10: The Customize Channel button allows you to make creative changes to your channel.

Figure 3-11: A pencil icon appears after you hover your mouse toward the right side of the screen on your Channel Overview page.

Figure 3-12: Change your trailer by clicking on For new visitors.

Figure 3-13: Click on Change trailer.

CHAPTER 04

Shooting Your Video

After you've got a good idea of what kind of video you're going to make and have an outline of what goes into that video, you're finally ready to shoot!

Chances are, if you are a new YouTuber, you may not have a lot of super expensive equipment to start out with. The good news is that you can still create amazing videos without spending a lot of money.

CHOOSING THE RIGHT CAMERA

You don't need to spend a lot of money to shoot a video for YouTube. You can use a basic webcam, smartphone, or digital camera.

A *webcam* is a camera that comes built into most computers and laptops. If your computer doesn't have one or you'd like to get an external webcam, you can easily find one online or at your local computer store.

Picking up a smartphone or tablet is just as good as using a digital camera for filming. With the advanced cameras and microphones on mobile devices, you can create stunning videos with minimal equipment.

You also may have access to a digital camera. If you don't already have a digital camera, I wouldn't recommend purchasing one until you'd like more professional-looking shots.

Webcams and mobile devices are the most common cameras used by beginners on YouTube. They both have high-definition (HD) capabilities, are easy to use, and mostly don't require another person.

USING WEBCAMS

Gamers, vloggers, reviewers, and more are among YouTubers who use webcams regularly and as their only video capture device. This is simply because using a webcam is the easiest way to record video, and it saves directly onto your computer. When you film on a smartphone or digital camera, you have to then upload the footage to your computer afterwards. With a webcam, the video is already on the computer and can be edited immediately.

Both Mac and Windows users can take advantage of their webcam to produce high-quality videos.

WINDOWS USERS

If you're a Windows user using an external webcam, make sure that it's plugged into a working USB port on your computer. When you plug in an external webcam for the first time, a pop-up window asks you to install any necessary drivers for your webcam so that it can communicate with your computer. Go ahead and follow the on-screen installation instructions.

After your external webcam is set up, you can follow these steps to take a photo or video:

1. **Click or tap on the search bar in the bottom-left corner of your Windows taskbar and type** Camera **to find the Camera app, shown in Figure 4-1.**

2. **Inside the app, click on the Camera button to take a still photo, shown in Figure 4-2.**

    Try taking a photo. Reposition your camera to your liking.

3. **To switch to video mode, use the small video camera icon just above the Camera button.**

    You can see the Camera button now turns into what looks like a video camera (see Figure 4-3). After you click on the video camera icon, you're ready to record video.

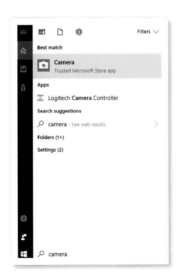

Figure 4-1: The Camera app for Windows.

Figure 4-2: The Camera button on the right side will take a still photo.

Figure 4-3: The video camera view.

The camera app on Windows 10 saves everything in a folder called Camera Roll. The Camera Roll folder is located inside the Pictures folder. To find your pictures and videos, go to File Explorer from your taskbar and then choose Pictures ⇨ Camera Roll.

MAC OS X USERS

What's really nice about Mac computers is that not only do they have a built-in HD webcam on all models, but no installation is required to begin using the webcam.

A good app to start with for beginners is Photo Booth.

To use Photo Booth to take a photo or video, follow these steps:

1. **In the top-right corner of your Mac, click on the Spotlight icon.**

   This icon looks like a magnifying glass. A shortcut key to open Spotlight is CMD + spacebar.

2. **Once the search bar appears, simply type** Photo Booth **(see Figure 4-4), and you can click on the icon to open.**

Figure 4-4: Typing **Photo Booth** into your Spotlight search bar accesses the program.

3. **To take a photo, click on the camera icon directly in the center of the application.**

   You see a nifty 3, 2, 1 countdown and snap! Your picture is taken. Figure 4-5 shows the Photo Booth app.

Figure 4-5: Inside the Photo Booth app.

4. **To record video, switch to video mode by clicking on the Film Strip icon.**

   You then see a red circle button that you can press to start recording video.

All of your photos and videos are saved directly in Photo Booth, so you can scroll through them right below the camera view. To export a photo or video, simply right-click on the photo or video that you want and then click on Export. Or, you can click and drag the image or video directly onto your desktop for easy access.

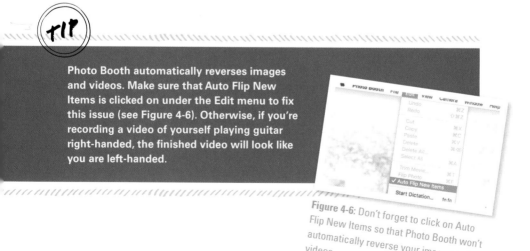

Photo Booth automatically reverses images and videos. Make sure that Auto Flip New Items is clicked on under the Edit menu to fix this issue (see Figure 4-6). Otherwise, if you're recording a video of yourself playing guitar right-handed, the finished video will look like you are left-handed.

Figure 4-6: Don't forget to click on Auto Flip New Items so that Photo Booth won't automatically reverse your images and videos.

TIPS AND TRICKS FOR WEBCAMS

No matter whether you're using a webcam on a Windows computer or a Mac, you can take advantage of a few tips and tricks to create the best possible images and videos:

- **Position your camera appropriately.** Center yourself in the middle of the shot or slightly off to one side. You do want to be the main view, so be sure to stay relatively close to the camera and make sure that the camera is in focus.

- **Clean your background.** Wherever you're shooting, tidy up the space. You don't want anything to unintentionally distract your viewer. Having garbage or clutter in the background can turn people away.

- **Take test shots.** Play around with both still and video settings with your webcam to get the ideal angle. When shooting video, speak in front of the camera to make sure the webcam is properly picking up your audio. If the audio sounds low or fuzzy, move closer to the camera and try again.

SHOOTING ON MOBILE

Mobile devices are great to use on the go. Whereas webcams are stationary by your computer, you can go anywhere with a smartphone or tablet. As a result, many vloggers, real-life adventurers, and reviewers use their smartphones to record their YouTube videos.

I'm going to assume that you already know how to open the camera application on your mobile device. If not, just look for an icon that resembles a camera, open it up, and experiment with the different options.

TIPS AND TRICKS FOR MOBILE DEVICES

The following tips and tricks can help you create the best possible images and videos on all types of mobile devices, including Androids, iPhones, and tablets:

- **Experiment with different settings.** If you see a flash icon, try using it and then disabling it. How did it affect your picture or video? When outside during the day, you generally do not need to use a flash.

- **Adjust the depth of field.** *Depth of field* is the distance between the closest and the furthest object in a photo. If you've ever seen a photo with an object up close and sharp-looking but the background is blurry, that has a shallow depth of field, meaning just a small portion of the image is in focus. This technique is used a lot to help focus on a particular subject or convey a certain message.

- **Focus.** To capture a clear image, tap on the screen where you'd like to focus before you take a picture or video. A box pops, which will adjust the focus. Get into the practice of adjusting the depth of field and focus to produce sharp results.

- **Consider using a selfie stick or tripod.** You can find inexpensive mounting devices to help with different shot types. Selfie sticks will provide a personal point of view, and a tripod can help establish a setting.

- **Remember to charge your mobile device!** When taking a mobile device out for a shoot, make sure that you have enough battery life. If not, bring a charger or external battery with you as backup. Recording video will eat away at your battery very quickly!

- **Film in landscape mode, not portrait.** Ever see a video with two large black panels taking up both sides? It was filmed in portrait mode, and that is exactly how you should not film on a smartphone.

  Turn your phone sideways, to *landscape mode*, for the best possible video quality. If you film in portrait mode, the video editing software that you use won't be able to flip the video, and you'll get those annoying black panels that you sometimes see in videos.

In portrait mode, you won't be able to remove the black panels on the sides when editing your video. This also comes off as unprofessional and sloppy-looking. In landscape mode, the clip looks much more professional and full.

Smartphone lens kits are super popular and very cost-effective. They typically come with a tripod and different lens attachments that you can attach to your smartphone.

UPPING YOUR GAME WITH DIGITAL CAMERAS

For those of you looking to step up your production game, using a digital camera will require more time, planning, and editing after you shoot. Purchasing a digital camera is an investment and requires care, however, so make sure that you're aware of the responsibilities that come with owning a digital camera.

TIPS AND TRICKS FOR DIGITAL CAMERAS

Digital cameras are pretty expensive for a beginner to go out and purchase right away, but if you already have one or are looking to buy, here are a few things to keep in mind:

- **Take good care of your digital camera.**   Owning a digital camera is a big responsibility, and in turn, you should treat it with care. Always keep the lens cap on when not in use to protect the lens. Buy a case for your camera if your budget allows and carry it with care.

- **Consider an SD card.**   An SD card is the place where all of your photos and videos get stored. Chances are, you'll have to purchase one with your camera. Always make sure that you have enough space on your SD card before shooting a video.

- **Be aware of your battery level.**   Be sure to always charge your digital camera before taking it out for a shoot. There's nothing worse than having your battery die while you're out filming.

- **Take test shots.**   Digital cameras have many settings to play around with. Don't be afraid to adjust the settings to see how you can adjust the camera to your liking.

USING SHOT ANGLES TO ADD INTEREST

You can use different angles to make your shots more eye-catching. This section covers how you can use different techniques to tell your story in a certain way. These shots can be done on a webcam, mobile device, or digital camera.

Close-up, medium, and wide angles are the most common shot types when shooting video. For most typical vlogs or gaming channels, these angles may not be necessary because your webcam will be stationed in one fixed position. However, if you're filming skits or other scenes, consider the following:

- A *wide angle shot* is shot from farther away showing an entire location, usually setting up scenery.

- A *medium shot* is a very common, standard level shot that usually shows the upper body of a subject.

- A *close-up shot* is used to get the viewer to focus only on what you have visible up close. These shots tend to be more dramatic and leave the viewer with not much else to focus on besides the subject.

Practice with a friend! Take a close-up, medium, and wide angle shot. Can you see how each shot can set up a scene differently? Use shot types to control what your viewer focuses on.

EVEN MORE SHOTS

In addition to the top three shots for understanding basic video, there are other ways YouTubers use different angles and shots tailored to their channel:

- *POV*, or *point-of-view*, shows what characters are seeing through their own eyes.

- A *high angle shot* has the viewer looking down from an upward position and can help make characters appear small, young, weak, childlike, confused, and so on.

- In a *low angle shot*, the camera is positioned below the character, looking up at them. This type of shot can help a character look bigger, stronger, or noble.

- Gamers always have a screengrab of the game they're playing and typically position their webcam video over it in one of the corners of the screen. Most gamers use OBS, Gameshow, or Xsplit, which are all really great, free-to-use broadcasting programs, to set up their gaming interface and even live stream.

PAYING ATTENTION TO LIGHTING

Lighting is very important because it can set a tone and create a mood. Darker lighting tends to have a scarier feel, while scenes outside in the sunlight are more bright and happy. Think about how you can use lighting to enhance your video.

PICKING UP AUDIO

For musicians and even someone just recording sound in general, you want to make sure that you have a good microphone or audio device. Viewers won't want to watch a video with poor sound quality.

For speech, you want to make sure that your viewers can clearly understand what you're saying at a moderate volume. They shouldn't have to turn up their volume all the way to hear you.

Also, make sure that the location where you're filming has little to no background noise. Background noises that can affect your video negatively include

- A loud fan or air-conditioning unit

- Outside noise, such as might be heard at a playground or on a busy street

- Other people chatting in the background

REMEMBER

You want your sound to be clean, clear, and without distraction.

TYPES OF MICROPHONES

Fortunately, the majority of webcams, mobile devices, and digital cameras have built-in microphones. If you're looking to get an external microphone for even better sound quality, here are a few options:

- **USB microphones:**   Similar to an external webcam, these external microphones plug directly into your computer. You can find USB microphones for cheap online, but high-quality USB microphones can cost $100 and up.

You would use a USB microphone only when recording video from your computer, such as a gamer or a vlogger does.

- **Smartphone microphone:** Dozens of cost-effective smartphone microphones will directly attach to your Android or iPhone device. They're light, portable, and easy to take with you on the go. (Depending on the type, a smartphone microphone attachment may drain the battery of the phone more quickly.)

- **Lavalier or lav microphone:** This small microphone clips onto your shirt and is primarily used for recording voice. It plugs directly into the audio port of digital cameras. You can purchase a lav relatively cheaply online.

- **Hot shoe microphone:** This type of microphone fits on the *hot shoe,* or top, of a digital camera. The company RØDE is known for making excellent hot shoe mics, but you'll have to be willing to spend about $60 and up to get a decent one. These microphones are ideal for capturing good, clean audio for subjects directly in front of the camera.

Want to learn about proper positioning for microphones? Check out this video on pickup patterns: http://bit.ly/2yQPIcK.

TESTING YOUR RECORDING

Do a sample recording inside. How does it sound? Is it clear? Any background noise? Try moving around into another room and observe any differences.

Next, if you're shooting on mobile or with a video camera, experiment shooting test scenes outside. What can you do to limit background noise?

Keep in mind how the sound may be impacted by the location you choose for your videos. Is it on a noisy street? Will you be inside a house with a loud AC unit? Think about any challenges that you may run into when planning your video location.

Doing a voiceover? Try recording in your closet! Believe it or not, the clothes inside a closet simulate sound absorption panels that are standard in recording studios. Closets are nice, quiet spaces that are great for recording audio!

PRACTICE MAKES PERFECT

If this is your first time shooting your own video, try not to overdo it. The only way you'll get better and learn is from practice. It's okay to make mistakes and that's how you learn for next time!

Try not to focus too hard on the details, or your overall message may get lost.

Also remember to save all of your takes and even the bad ones! You may find out that some of your bad takes can be usable in other ways!

CHAPTER

05

Editing

In this chapter, you'll find out about the best practices for editing so that you can easily make awesome, professional-looking videos ready to upload! You can apply the techniques covered in this chapter to any program you choose to edit in.

Just a heads up: The screenshots in this chapter are all from iMovie, which is downloadable for free on a Mac.

IMPORTING FOOTAGE

Before you import, you'll want all of your footage in one spot so that you can easily skim through and decide what's usable!

Quickly go through all your video clips and trash any that aren't good. Oftentimes, you'll find accidental .01 second clips of your shoes or bad takes that you don't want! Also, get rid of any bad-looking takes with poor color or lighting. You'll save a ton of time by trashing these before importing.

In addition to all usable video files, be sure to also import any still images, audio clips, and music that you want to use in the video, too.

Keep in mind that organization is key. It's a good idea to have all your project files in one single folder to stay organized. This way, you aren't scrambling all over the place looking for files (see Figure 5-1).

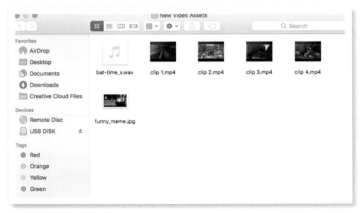

Figure 5-1: A folder containing images, videos, and audio samples.

A *digital asset* is any video, image, sound, or usable file that is included in a project. In the case of video-making, you want to make sure that all of your assets are organized and in one place so that you can easily access them when editing. This way, when it comes time to edit, every file you want to use is in one spot!

Depending on what software you're using to edit your video, you most likely either have to drag and drop your files into the program or simply use the standard File⇨Import technique. (Refer to Figure 5-2).

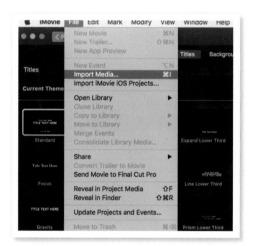

Figure 5-2: Importing files in iMovie.

After you import all your assets, make sure that within your video-editing program the project is properly labeled to go with the title of your video.

CUTTING CLIPS

When you're ready to edit, drop all of your usable clips, in order, onto the timeline (see Figure 5-3). Just grab chunks of clips at a time and don't worry about cutting them just yet. Right now, you want to focus on finding all clips that have the potential to be used in the project.

Figure 5-3: Dragging all usable clips onto the timeline.

After you have everything in place, you're ready edit. Here are a few tips:

- Start by checking the beginning and ending of each clip because those usually need to be trimmed down first.

- Make sure that you aren't cutting out any dialogue.

- Check the timings of each clip to make sure there isn't too quick of a cut or too long of a moment between.

A *quick cut* is a series of clips, usually three seconds or less, used in a row. YouTubers tend to use quick cuts and fast edits as a technique to accent a point or add comedic effect to a video. Try experimenting with a quick-cut technique in your video.

ADDING TEXT, TRANSITIONS, AND AUDIO

After you organize the clips in your timeline, you're ready to add some fun stuff. Titles and transitions are optional, but recommended to use when editing a video. Just like audio, they can really jazz it up and add personality!

TEXT

While text is always fun to add in to a video, don't overuse it. In most video editing software, adding text to your project is referred to as a *title*. Do not confuse adding a title while video editing with the actual title, or name, of your video.

You can add titles, or text, to any part of your project. Most YouTubers will add text in the beginning, sometimes during the middle to stress a point, and often at the end of the video to wrap things up.

You can use text and titles for

- Narrating a video with just text

- Labeling things, such as a places, people, and events

- Transitional moments between scenes, such as "Six months later . . ."

- Credits at the end of a video

Try to think of other reasons you would want to add text to your video. Will this text enhance the quality of your viewer's experience?

Be sure that the font you use for your text is easy to read. You want your font to fit seamlessly into the video and not serve as a distraction. Ask yourself

- Is it easy to read?

- Is it large enough?

- Will it distract my viewers?

As shown in Figure 5-4, under the Titles screen in iMovie, you can drag the particular text title you'd like to use directly onto a video clip in your timeline.

Scan through all the different font choices in your software and choose one you think looks good!

Figure 5-4: Adding text to your video project.

TRANSITIONS

A *transition* is a feature you can use while video editing that nicely ties two separate clips together.

You can add lots of fun transitions in between clips, but don't get too carried away. Some transitions are really playful, whereas others tend to fit a more dramatic mood. For example, if you have a serious video that you're trying to edit, using a disco ball transition probably won't fit the mood very well.

I challenge you to watch three random YouTube videos and take notice what transitions are used between clips. I bet you'll be surprised to see how often transitions are used between clips!

TYPES OF TRANSITIONS

Transitions lead the viewer from one clip to another. Especially if you're changing scenes, a nice transition can really help enhance the flow of your video. Without a transition in between clips, a change of scenery can appear to be abrupt and disturb the viewer's immersion into your video.

Here are some examples of commonly used, subtle transitions that really enhance the flow of your video:

- **Dissolves**: Also referred to as a Cross-Dissolve, this transition takes two clips and seamlessly mixes them together where your next clip blends with your previous clip in the timeline. It's very subtle and used very commonly in video editing.

It helps suggest a change of locations or even a passing of time.

- **Fade In/Fade Out**: Fades are a bit more dramatic than a dissolve where the beginning of your clip will fade in from black, or the end of your clip will slowly dim to black. Fades can create an element of suspense or drama.

- **The Wipe**: Many wipe transition effects exist, but some of them can come off as vintage or even a bit corny. Wipes start with some sort of shape and move through your video clip — almost like turning the page of a book — and dissolve into the next scene. Use wipes on light, nonserious, or dramatic subject matter.

No matter what transition you decide to use between clips, keep it consistent. If you decide on using a dissolve, then I recommend you use a Dissolve for all of your transitions.

Be careful! Sometimes transitions cut off the beginning and ending of clips that they're placed between. Double-check after applying your transition that the clips before and after aren't affected.

AUDIO

Music can really help set the tone of a video. Is your channel fun and exciting? Look for music that will reflect that mood.

You must be careful when choosing music because YouTube is very strict about copyright policies! Any music that you do not own or create is not your property and therefore is eligible to get flagged when you use it in a YouTube video. To avoid this issue, I recommend using *royalty-free music,* which simply means that anyone can use this music without getting in trouble.

YouTube has its own audio library with all royalty-free music that you can download and use in your videos. In the audio library (se Figure 5-5), you can select length, genre, mood, and much more.

After you decide on appropriate music, play your video back from the beginning to make sure that the audio isn't too loud. If your video has dialogue, you want to make sure the speech is loud and clear and that the music in the background complements the mood. Just like titles, you don't want the music to be too loud and distracting to your viewers. Play around with the different sound levels to see what fits best. Try listening back with your computer speakers and then try again with headphones.

Figure 5-5: YouTube's royalty-free audio library with songs you can download to use for your videos at www.youtube.com/audiolibrary/music.

For some advanced audio settings, you can adjust your bitrate. *Bitrate* simply refers to the amount of data, or bits, that can be processed at a time. In the case of audio, the higher the bitrate, the better quality audio you'll have.

For specific bitrate settings, make sure that the audio bitrate is either

- 128 kbps for Mono

- 384 kbps for Stereo

- 512 kbps for 5.1 surround

REVIEWING AND EXPORTING

When you think your video is all set, watch it from start to finish just to make sure no final edits need to be made. Continue making any last-minute changes and edits until you're completely satisfied with the content.

After you're happy, you're ready to export your video. Most programs have a File ⇨ Export or File ⇨ Share option. After you export or share your video, a final screen appears (see Figure 5-6). There, you name your project and tinker with any last-minute settings, and then you're good to go!

Figure 5-6: Export your video file from iMovie.

USING DIFFERENT FILE FORMATS FOR VIDEO

You can upload a variety of different file formats for video. Just to be sure your video is in an acceptable format; the following are accepted by YouTube:

- .3GPP: A file format that mostly originates from mobile devices

- .AVI: A very common, standard video format

- .FLV: Short for flash video, a compressed video format

- MP4: A compressed format for a Mac computer

- .MPEG4: Another compressed format for Mac computers

- .MOV: A QuickTime video file, standard on a Mac computer

- WebM: A compressed format optimized for web use

- .WMV: Windows Media Video, standard on a Windows computer

If you try to upload a different type of file format other than those listed, you'll get an error message from YouTube. If your video is stuck in a certain file format, try an online search for a free video converter, and you'll be able to change the file format to one acceptable by YouTube.

EXPLORING ADVANCED EXPORT SETTINGS

Don't feel like you need to use advanced export settings, if you don't want to. However, if you want to explore these settings, then this section is for you.

FPS, or frames per second, is the number of times a single frame of video is displayed per second. The higher your FPS, the smoother your video will appear.

Make sure that you edit your video in the same frame rate (or FPS) that it was recorded in. Standard frame rates are 24, 25, 30, 48, 50, and 60 frames per second.

Also, Table 5-1 shows you a handy chart on video Mbps. Mbps stands for *megabits per second,* a measure of data transfer speed. Similar to bitrate, the higher the Mbps, the better quality the video will be!

A *resolution* is the number of pixels visible on your screen. Standard high-definition resolution is 1080p, where the p is short for *pixels.*

Table 5-1 is a handy chart that shows what mbps is recommended depending on your current resolution.

Table 5-1 Video Mbps

Resolution	Megabits per second
360p	1 Mbps
480p	2.5 Mbps
720p	5 Mbps
1080p	8 Mbps
1440p (2k)	16 Mbps
2160p (4k)	35-45 Mbps

YouTube can currently support up to 4K or 2160p video resolution, which is one of the current highest resolutions available to consumers.

LOOKING AT VIDEO-EDITING SOFTWARE

You can use so many different programs to edit videos. If you're just starting out with YouTube, I recommend going with a free program or a software that is already installed on your computer.

MAC

Here are a couple of easy accessible programs for Mac:

- **iMovie:** You can use iMovie for free on any Mac computer. It's simple to use for beginners, yet has very powerful features that can make your videos look really professional!

- **Final Cut Pro X:** Final Cut Pro X, or FCPX, is an industry-level professional video-editing software. It'll cost you a few hundred bucks if you want to purchase it. I recommend FCPX for those who are serious, advanced video makers. It's not too difficult to learn how to use, and most of the interface has a drag-and-drop format. On the downside, it's pretty pricey at $299.99.

You can download both iMovie and Final Cut Pro X from the App Store on your Mac.

WINDOWS (PC)

Here are a few accessible programs for Windows:

- **Easy Movie Maker:** Easy Movie Maker is a free program that you can download for your Windows computer. Geared toward beginners, it's very easy to learn and has lots of features to make really great-looking videos. You can download easy Movie Maker from the Microsoft Store on your Windows Computer.

- **HitFilm Express:** HitFilm Express is a completely free video editing and VFX software. It's a bit more advanced than Easy Movie Maker, and it also has features that you can pay to unlock. You can find out more about HitFilm Express at https://hitfilm.com/express.

CHAPTER

06

Uploading Your Video

Your video is complete and ready to upload. So what's the next step? Uploading!

In this chapter, I cover the best practices for uploading your video to YouTube by going over titling, description, thumbnails, and more. I even give you an Upload Checklist that you can bookmark or print so that you don't forget anything!

YOUR UPLOAD CHECKLIST

Uploading your video isn't as simple as just uploading it. The uploading process requires several tasks:

- Upload your video

- Create your title

- Write a description of your video

- Add tags

- Upload a thumbnail

- Add End screen & Annotations

- Create subtitles

Figure 6-1 is a handy checklist that you can print and mark off during the uploading process.

UPLOAD CHECKLIST

- ☐ UPLOAD VIDEO
- ☐ CRAFT CATCHY TITLE
- ☐ WRITE DESCRIPTION USING KEYWORDS
- ☐ ADD TAGS
- ☐ UPLOAD THUMBNAIL
- ☐ ADD END SCREEN ANNOTATIONS
- ☐ SUBTITLES

Figure 6-1: An Upload checklist.

UPLOADING YOUR VIDEO TO YOUTUBE

After you create a video, you're ready to upload it to YouTube. Go to www.youtube.com/upload (see Figure 6-2). Just make sure that you're logged in to your account. Once there, click on the center icon to upload your video.

Figure 6-2: Your video upload screen.

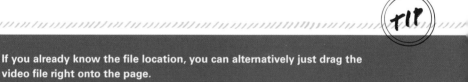

If you already know the file location, you can alternatively just drag the video file right onto the page.

FINDING EVERYTHING YOU NEED IN INFO & SETTINGS

Absolutely everything that you need after you upload your video is found under Info & Settings. You're automatically directed to this page after your video is finished uploading.

Some of the things you'll be particularly interested in doing in this area include

- Creating titles

- Writing descriptions

- Tagging your video

- Using thumbnails

- Scheduling videos

- Creating a playlist

The following sections explore each feature of the Info & Settings screen.

CRAFTING GREAT TITLES

While the video is uploading (see Figure 6-3), you can fill out the title field. Creating a catchy title isn't easy, and it can make the difference in someone deciding to watch your video.

Figure 6-3: The upload progress screen where you can begin to enter in title, description, and tags to your video.

But what causes a title to show up in a search? A trick YouTubers do for help is to use YouTube's built-in search suggestion tool for better titles and tags.

The search suggestion is what comes up in YouTube midway while you're typing something. It's often used to autocomplete whatever you're typing.

REMEMBER

The most important thing to keep in mind is to craft a title that will show up in search results.

The search suggestions results are currently, in order, the top ranking searches on YouTube based on the keyword you were typing. Figure 6-4 shows the top search results that most people seek when they type **Pokémon Go** into YouTube.

Figure 6-4: YouTube search suggestions.

Follow these additional tips for creating great titles:

- Use an accurate, but brief, description in the title. Don't make it too long!

- Try to incorporate at least one of the YouTube search suggestions in the title of your video to increase its searchability. So, if your video is a review of your experience playing the game Pokémon Go, the good news is that Pokémon Go is one of the top searches!

  For example, a title like "Pokémon Go App Review 2017" would work just fine. It's short, accurate, and right to the point.

Experiment with different titling techniques in your videos and see what works best. Another method to try is to make the title a bit of a tease or sneak-peak to encourage viewers to want to watch. "What I found playing Pokémon Go!" or "My Top 5 Pokémon Go Places" are open-ended titles that pique curiosity.

WRITING A GOOD DESCRIPTION

Like your title, a good video description is very important to include. Your description should perfectly describe what your video is about. It should also include an invitation for the viewer to subscribe to your channel.

A well-worded description will help viewers find your channel. Any words that you use in it have the ability to show up in a YouTube search result. It's a very useful area for viewers to learn about your video and choose whether or not they'd like to watch it.

Make sure each of your videos has their own unique description.

Including the title of your video somewhere in the description, too, is always good.

For example, if you've created a Pokémon Go review video, be sure to fill out the description accurately. A good start is

My review of the game Pokémon Go in 2017. This video will cover what's new, what has been changed, and why I like the game. Hope you enjoy!

Be sure to subscribe to my channel for more game reviews here: www.youtube.com/*your_channel_name_here*

TAGGING YOUR VIDEO

Tags help viewers find your videos when they search for particular words in a YouTube search. When uploading your video, you add tags underneath your description field.

Properly tagging your video will greatly help boost your video's ability to show up in search results. Be sure to use any words describing your video you can think of off the top of your head. Think about certain words that would help your video show up in a search.

For example, if your video is "Pokémon Go App Review," some potential tags include Pokémon, Pokémon go, game, app, review, changes, updates, news, and 2017.

If you mention any specific Pokémon in the video, you should include them in the tags as well.

REMEMBER

If you mention another channel, website, or anything outside of your YouTube page, it's always a good idea to credit or add a link to your description. For example:

For more information on Pokémon Go, visit its website at www. pokemongo.com.

Use the YouTube search suggestion feature to see popular search terms and whether any of them can apply to your own video tags! (For more on this feature, see the section "Crafting great titles," earlier in this chapter.)

ATTRACTING VIEWERS WITH THUMBNAILS

When you search for a video on YouTube, what do you look for? What is it that stands out that makes you want to watch a video?

Most people would say either the title or thumbnail. Having a thumbnail that really pops can make the difference in a viewer's decision to watch your video.

A nice thumbnail attracts more people to your video, but it must also accurately describe the point of the video in a catchy way.

After your video is finished processing, you'll be able to upload your own custom thumbnail. If you've got your own custom thumbnail ready to go, see the following instructions on how to upload it. If you don't have one just yet, refer to the next section to read about the science behind a good thumbnail.

REMEMBER

Save any changes you make to your video before changing screens.

1. **Go to the main video-editing screen.**

2. **Click on your channel icon in the upper-right of the screen.**

3. **Click on Creator Studio, as shown in Figure 6-5.**
   Your Dashboard appears.

4. **Find the video on your Dashboard and click on Edit (see Figure 6-6).**

   Your main edit page appears. Take a look at the series of still images next to your video (see Figure 6-7). YouTube automatically generates these thumbnails. You can choose to use one of these images or upload your own custom one.

5. **To upload your own custom thumbnail, highlight your cursor over the last thumbnail, which is on the bottom of the list (see Figure 6-7).**

6. **Click on Change image to upload your custom image.**

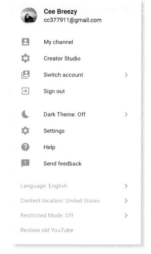

Figure 6-5: Click on Creator Studio.

TIP

Does your account say you can't upload custom thumbnails? That may be because your account isn't verified with YouTube. To verify your account, simply go to www.youtube.com/verify and fill out the information.

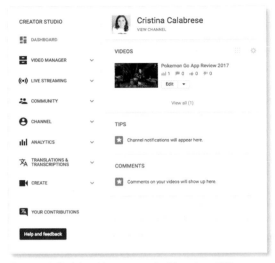

Figure 6-6: Find the video on your dashboard you'd like to edit.

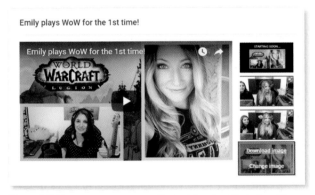

Figure 6-7: Hover your mouse over the last thumbnail listed next to your video to upload your own custom thumbnail.

Figures 6-8 and 6-9 show two examples of thumbnails for a video called "Pokémon Go App Review 2017." Which one would you say is better?

Figure 6-8 has really small, plain-looking text, and the images don't really blend well together.

Figure 6-9 uses a similar color scheme to the actual Pokémon logo in a big, bright font. The positioning of the text looks natural and stands out when added to the background image. Figure 6-9 would have a way better chance of standing out on YouTube.

Figure 6-8: A very basic thumbnail.

Figure 6-9: A thumbnail with a little more effort put into it.

Here are a few tips to help you create good thumbnails:

- **Add large, but brief, text.** Don't overdo it on text. A few words to describe the video will do.

- **Choose popping colors and images.** Use an image and color that will attract someone's eye.

- **Create thumbnails that look good both large and small.** YouTube search results vary in sizes based on what you're browsing with: smartphone, computer, tablet, and so on. Make sure your thumbnail looks good on both a large and small screen.

- **Use fun, bold fonts.** Large, fat fonts are popular on YouTube. Try experimenting with different fonts types to see what could really stand out!

Try an online search for "free fonts" to download some cool fonts that you can use when creating your thumbnail.

SCHEDULING AND ADDING PRIVACY

Sometimes you don't want to always publish your videos right away. Your upload page gives you a way to schedule videos to premiere on a certain date and time.

On the upload main page for your video, use the drop-down menu on the right side to schedule and set your privacy level (see Figure 6-10).

You can't schedule a video that has already been published.

Figure 6-10: Set the privacy for your video.

Your options include

- **Public:** Anyone can view the video on YouTube.

- **Unlisted:** Only people you share the link with can view the video. It's not searchable on YouTube.

- **Private:**   You're the only one who can view the video.

- **Scheduled:**   You can select the date and time for the video to be published in the future as a public video.

CREATE A PLAYLIST

A *playlist* is a series of videos organized in one spot. You can make a playlist of your favorite videos on YouTube, or you can make playlists on your own channel for viewers to easily navigate. Think of it as an organized collection of videos.

Here's how you make a playlist:

1. **Click on +Add to playlist (see Figure 6-11) while under the Edit portion of your video.**

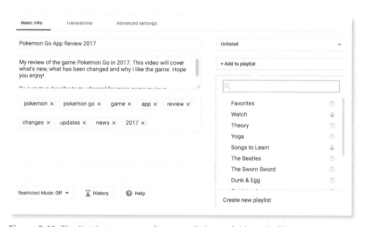

Figure 6-11: The list that pops up after you click on +Add to playlist.

2. **From the list that appears, click on Create new playlist.**

3. **In the screen that appears, title your playlist and choose its visibility (public, unlisted, or private).**

4. **Click on Create.**

   Your playlist is created.

TIP

You can always change privacy settings of playlists as well as videos, making them private, public, and unlisted.

EXPLORING ADVANCED FEATURES

A few more advanced features can help enhance your video after you've uploaded it:

- Enhancements

- Audio

- End screen & Annotations

- Cards

- Subtitles/CC

You can access all the features in this section after you click on Edit for any of your videos through your dashboard.

ENHANCEMENTS

The Enhancement screen is a great tool that lets you easily make some visual changes to your video. In this screen, you can auto-fix light and color in your video, change the speed, trim the video, and more.

AUDIO

If you upload a video without audio, you can add music from YouTube's royalty-free library.

REMEMBER

If you do make any changes that you aren't happy with, you can always click on Revert to Original to get back to normal.

Royalty-free means that you won't have any copyright issues using the audio in your video because you're using someone else's work without permission.

Within this audio section, you can scroll through different tracks, lengths and genres to overlay audio to your video.

If you have dialogue, using this feature will overwrite your voice. Only use this feature if you want only background music in your video!

END SCREEN & ANNOTATIONS

Ever watch something on YouTube and see clickable videos at the end? These *end screens* encourage people to keep watching your videos and stay on your channel.

An end screen can include links to

- Your other videos
- Your playlists
- Your channel
- Your website

The annotation will automatically start about ten seconds before the end of your video.

I strongly recommend that you use end screens after all of your videos because it's a great way to keep a viewer engaged in your content.

To apply an end screen:

1. **After your uploaded video is finished processing, click on End screen & Annotations from your upload page (see Figure 6-12).**

   You see the screen in which you can add in an end screen.

Figure 6-12: The End screen & Annotations section when editing a video.

2. **To apply an annotation, click on Use template (see Figure 6-13).**

   A screen appears where you can now choose a template.

Figure 6-13: Clicking on Use template allows you to choose a preformatted annotation to apply to your video.

3. **Click on the template that looks suitable for your video and then click on Select (see Figure 6-14).**

   Your chosen template now appears over your video.

4. **Click on the pencil icon and then click on Edit element so that you can select what you'd like to do with each element (see Figure 6-15).**

   You can resize the elements as well as drag them around to a different portion of your video. Most people link their other videos or playlists.

5. **Save your progress after you're finished.**

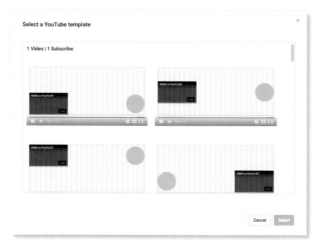

Figure 6-14: Choose a template for your End screen & Annotations.

CARDS

A *card* is a link you can add to your video that will direct viewers to a specific video or URL. Say that you reference another one of your videos. You can simply add a card that viewers can click on to view that referenced video.

To add a card:

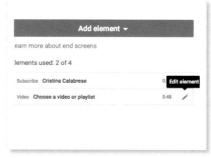

Figure 6-15: Edit element allows you to customize what type of link you want in your annotation.

1. **Click on Add Card.**

   A list appears with several options (see Figure 6-16).

2. **Click on the type of card you want.**

   You can choose from a

   • Video or Playlist

   • Poll

   • Link

   In this example, I walk you through choosing a video.

3. **To add a card linking another video, click on Create.**

Figure 6-16: The different types of cards you can add to your video.

4. **In the screen that appears, select which video you'd like.**

5. **Click on Create card.**

   Your card now appears under your video.

6. **Drag the card into a specific time in your video where you'd like it to appear.**

SUBTITLES/CC

YouTube can detect language in your video and provide auto-generated subtitles, or closed captioning. If you have a script written, it's a great idea to add Subtitles/CC to your video to increase the range of people who can view your video. Adding Subtitles/CC is great for those who are hearing impaired have trouble understanding verbal English, or would just prefer to read along to your dialogue.

Adding subtitles is simple:

1. **Click on the Subtitles/CC section.**

2. **Click on the blue button that says "Add new subtitles or CC" and then click on your desired language, as shown in Figure 6-17.**

3. **Click on Transcribe and auto-sync (see Figure 6-18) from the options of subtitle methods.**

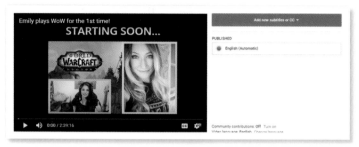

Figure 6-17: You can add subtitles to your video.

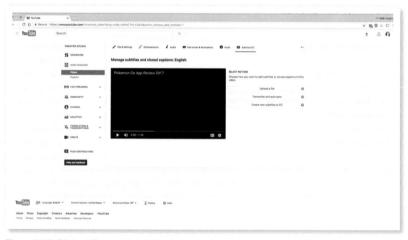

Figure 6-18: Click on Transcribe and auto-sync.

4. **Copy and paste your script inside the video transcript box, shown in Figure 6-19.**

   The video transcript box will convert your script into subtitles.

5. **Click on Set timings.**

   It may take a few minutes, but YouTube takes the script that you've pasted into the box and sets the timings automatically.

6. **Under My Drafts, click on your draft after it no longer says Setting timings.**

Figure 6-19: The video transcript box.

7. **In the window that appears, preview the video with the subtitles and make any changes (see Figure 6-20).**

8. **Save your changes when finished.**

Figure 6-20: Preview your subtitles to ensure the timing is correct.

ACCESSING YOUR VIDEOS THROUGH VIDEO MANAGER

The place where you can quickly access all your videos for editing is the Video Manager. The Video Manager allows you to make changes, organize, and view all your uploaded videos in one place.

To access Video Manager:

1. **From anywhere on YouTube, make sure that you're logged in and then click on your channel icon in the upper-right side of the screen.**

2. **On the menu that appears, click on Creator Studio.**

3. **Click on Video Manager.**

   The Video Manager appears.

Familiarize yourself by navigating around the Video Manager so that you can feel comfortable making changes and edits to your videos easily.

CHAPTER

07

Sharing Your Video

Sharing your video helps increase its visibility. In this chapter, I go over a few ways you can do so to get some more views.

ENCOURAGING FRIENDS

There's no harm in asking your friends to check out your channel. Friends are sometimes the best way you can get honest feedback on your work. Ask a few friends to

REMEMBER

Sometimes having a fresh set of eyes on your videos is the best way to improve your channel. Ask for opinions often! Don't be afraid of constructive criticism — you should welcome it! Constructive criticism will help you along your journey.

- Check out your channel

- Watch a video

- Tell you what they think

- Subscribe to your channel

- Share it with their friends

These are just some things that a friend can do to help with your channel — especially if you're just starting out. By providing their honest opinion, your friends can give you a perspective that you may not see yourself as the creator of the content.

EXTENDING BEYOND YOUTUBE

So your video is shared on YouTube. Now what? You can sit around and see whether it'll stack up views, or you can be more proactive and try sharing it elsewhere!

LINKING ACROSS MULTIPLE PLATFORMS

Many of my friends who also run YouTube channels share their work on all their social media accounts, including but not limited to

- Facebook
- Twitter
- Instagram

FACEBOOK

Pasting a link to your video will embed the video in your post so that people on Facebook can click on the Play button directly. Facebook also opens up a whole new audience outside of YouTube. All your Facebook friends have the potential to view, like, comment, and share your video.

Because these links on Facebook are linked to your original YouTube video, even though the video plays from Facebook, it will still count as a view on YouTube.

TWITTER

Similar to Facebook, Twitter allows you to paste a link to your video directly in a tweet. After you tweet your post, a preview of your video appears and gives the user the option to play your video directly from your tweet.

REMEMBER

Don't forget to add a couple of appropriate #hashtags in the tweet!

Because these links on Twitter are linked to your original YouTube video, even though the video plays from Twitter, it will still count as a view on YouTube.

INSTAGRAM

You can't directly link YouTube videos on Instagram, but here are a few tips to utilize this platform:

- Go to edit your profile and under Website, link your latest video.

- In the description field, you can write something like "Check out my latest YT video in the link below!" (Refer to Figure 7-1.)

- Post the image of your video's thumbnail on Instagram and encourage viewers to check the link in your profile to see the latest video.

- Include hashtags in your post that would relate to your video.

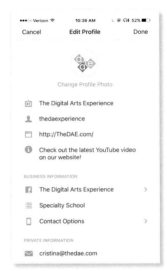

Figure 7-1: The Instagram Edit Profile screen on a mobile device.

Instagram has a limit of 30 hashtags, so don't be afraid to add some to increase the reach of your post. Need ideas for hashtags? Use some of the tags that you've added to your video (see Chapter 6).

RAISING AWARENESS ON SIMILAR YOUTUBE CHANNELS

Self-promoting yourself in the comments of someone else's YouTube channel is generally looked down upon. (Refer to Figure 7-2) In fact, soliciting usually gets your comment removed or banned from a channel.

However, you can use a few other techniques to raise awareness of your channel without directly saying "Hey, check out my channel!"

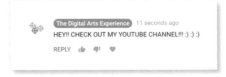

Figure 7-2: A great example of what not to write.

Start small by finding five channels that are similar to yours. Subscribe to them. Check out their videos. Don't be afraid to write down ideas! If you enjoy one of their videos, like the video and write a comment. By commenting on a video, other viewers will have the chance to see your username and check out your channel.

COLLABORATING WITH OTHERS

The act of working together with someone else toward a similar goal is *collaboration.*

REMEMBER

Don't comment unless it's genuine! If you write an interesting comment, people are more likely to reply to it and check out your channel. This is a workaround for soliciting on other channels.

Working with other YouTubers is a great way to help expand your reach. But in order to create a nice collaboration, you'll need to think about what types of channels would complement your own.

For example, if you run a music channel where you feature your own original songs as well as cover songs, what types of channels could you collaborate with? Here are a few ideas:

- **Other musicians:** What better way for musicians to expose their music to more audiences than to collaborate with other musicians? Creating or covering a song that features both of you is a great way to work on a project together that you can share with both of your audiences.

- **Special FX/video production:** Do you know a video person — someone who is really into making nicely produced short films? You can work together to film a music video for your channel. Your music, their video work — it's a great way to show off the strengths of both channels.

- **Audio gear reviewers:** Got a favorite type of microphone for your music channel? Perhaps you can find a YouTuber who reviews microphones and other audio gear and then feature it in a new song for your channel. Not a bad way to cross-promote a product and then showcase it!

- **Music reviewers:** Many YouTubers love doing reviews! You can search for channels that feature and review up-and-coming musicians on YouTube. Getting your work featured on a music review channel is a great way to expand the reach of your content.

These ideas are just a few ways you can collaborate with other YouTubers to help your channel gain more attention.

I wouldn't recommend trying to collaborate with other YouTubers until you've established your channel and have a decent following.

RECOGNIZING THE IMPORTANCE OF SUBSCRIBERS

Your goal when starting out should be to get more subscribers. The larger the following you have, the more views your videos will get, giving your channel more of a chance to grow.

UNDERSTANDING WHY SUBSCRIBERS ARE CRITICAL TO SUCCESS

YouTube will tell you that your subscribers have the tendency to watch way more of your content than nonsubscribers. The reason this fact is important is that channels with higher watch times have a better chance of showing up in search results.

Subscribers are the first people to get notified whenever you upload a new video. The more subscribers you have, the more views your videos will get as they first go live, which increases the searchability of your videos. Make sense?

Additionally, when you get more subscribers, extra features for your YouTube channel will unlock.

INVITING VIEWERS

At the end of each video, you should invite your viewers to subscribe to your channel. Don't be too forceful or annoying about it. People will want to subscribe on their own will, not because they felt pressured into it. But, viewers who do enjoy your content are more likely to subscribe.

Many YouTubers provide a direct link in their video description to sub-scribe to their channel. An easy way to do so is to use this link:

```
www.youtube.com/subscription_center?add_user=your_
    username_here
```

In the preceding link, replace *your_username_here* with your own channel name. Is your channel name WackyBananas765? Then your link should look like

```
www.youtube.com/subscription_center?add_user=
    WackyBananas765
```

Want to hide your subscribers until you get to a number that looks good? Make sure you're logged into your YouTube account. Here's what you need to do:

1. **In the upper-right corner of your screen, click on your channel icon.**

   A list of options appears (see Figure 7-3).

2. **Click on Creator Studio, where you'll be brought to your channel's dashboard with many options to choose from.**

3. **Click on Channel in the left panel.**

   You're immediately given more options for your channel.

4. **Click on Advanced (see Figure 7-4).**

5. **In the Subscriber counts section, shown in Figure 7-5, choose whether you'd like to have your subscriber count visible to the public.**

6. **Click on Save.**

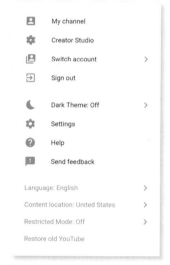

Figure 7-3: A list of channel options, including Creator Studio.

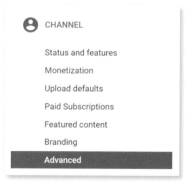

Figure 7-4: Your Channel section where you can find Advanced settings.

Subscriber counts

● Display the number of people subscribed to my channel

○ Do not display the number of people subscribed to my channel

Figure 7-5: The Subscriber counts section.

MAKING GOOD VIDEOS

This goes without saying, but I'm going to say it anyway. No one will subscribe to your channel unless you have good quality content.

A good general rule I use is to ask myself "Is this something I would watch?"

Be highly critical of your work. If you're taking the time to create something, you want it to be the best it could possibly be. Don't settle for mediocre content. If you think your video isn't good, why would a stranger on YouTube think it is?

Why would someone want to subscribe to your channel? Make it worth their time by providing value and good, original content. Don't be afraid to ask your viewers questions. You can even set up a poll card (see Chapter 6) in videos to get feedback. Subscribers can give you ideas for new content and tell you what they like. Listening to your subscribers can really help shape your channel and drive it in the right direction!

CHAPTER

08

Tracking Your Video Performance

In this chapter, I talk about YouTube analytics. I'm not going to specifically go through each and every feature of YouTube analytics — I want you to explore each section on your own — but I do give you an overview of some of the main things to look for that will help improve your channel.

ACCESSING YOUTUBE ANALYTICS

A huge part of growing your channel is studying your analytics. *Analytics* are detailed stats viewable for each of your videos. They can show you how your videos are performing, who is watching your videos, how long they're watching them, where your viewers are coming from, and many, many more awesome stats.

To access your Analytics page, make sure you're logged in to your YouTube account and then follow these steps:

1. **In the upper-right corner of your screen, click on your channel icon.**

   A list of options appears (see Figure 8-1).

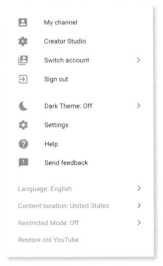

Figure 8-1: A list of channel options, including Creator Studio.

2. **Click on Creator Studio.**

   You see your channel's dashboard, which has many options for you to choose from.

3. **Click on Analytics on the left side of the screen.**

   You now see your Analytics page (see Figure 8-2).

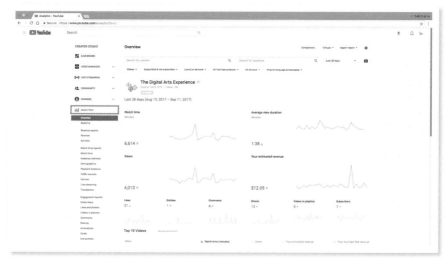

Figure 8-2: An overview of your YouTube Analytics page.

BREAKING DOWN THE NUMBERS

These analytics can be very confusing at first, so don't get overwhelmed if you don't understand all of them right away. Your analytics are divided into sections so that you can view them more easily. Each section has its own categories:

- Overview and Realtime

- Revenue reports

- Watch time reports

- Engagement reports

The following sections go over each category, shown in Figure 8-3, in detail.

Figure 8-3: Each category in YouTube analytics.

OVERVIEW AND REALTIME

By default, whenever you click on Overview, YouTube will show you an overview of your entire channel over the past 28 days. Now, don't get overwhelmed by first visiting this page. There's a lot of information and a lot of things to look at and click on.

To access the Overview page for a specific video:

1. **On the Overview page, click on the Search for Content box (see Figure 8-4).**

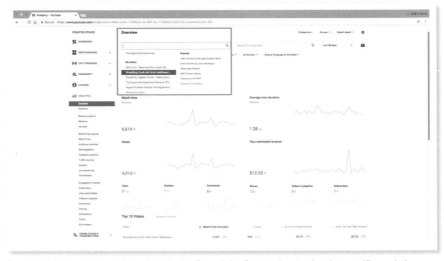

Figure 8-4: You can search for a video in the Search for Content box to view its specific analytics.

2. **Type your video title or select one of the suggestions that appears.**

   The Overview page for that specific video appears.

By default, you see the following reports, as shown in Figure 8-5:

- Watch time

- Average view duration

- Views

- Your estimated revenue

- Top geographics

- Gender

- Traffic sources

- Playback locations

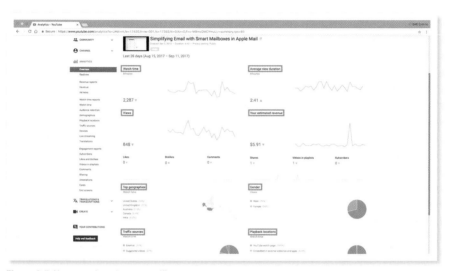

Figure 8-5: You can view these specific reports.

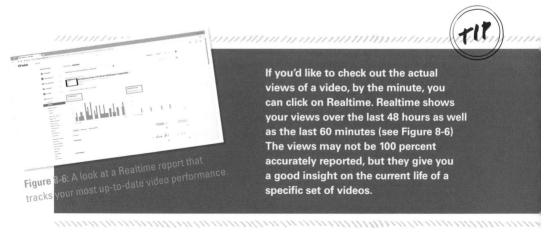

Figure 8-6: A look at a Realtime report that tracks your most up-to-date video performance.

If you'd like to check out the actual views of a video, by the minute, you can click on Realtime. Realtime shows your views over the last 48 hours as well as the last 60 minutes (see Figure 8-6) The views may not be 100 percent accurately reported, but they give you a good insight on the current life of a specific set of videos.

REVENUE REPORTS

Your revenue reports track how much money your channel is making from advertisements. These reports will be active only if you've set up your channel for monetization. (Monetization is covered in Chapter 9, so if you're interested in learning how to make money off your videos, please check that out.)

Your revenue reports are broken down into three parts:

- Revenue

- Transaction revenue

- Ad rates

REVENUE

Revenue refers to the overall amount of money your account has made via transaction revenue and ad rates.

The amount you see listed in your analytics is an estimate that is updated on the 15th of every month.

TRANSACTION REVENUE

Transaction revenue is money that you've made through fan funding or paid content. As your channel grows and you unlock more features, you'll be able to receive money, or donations, from viewers.

An example of fan funding is money that you receive through something called Super Chat. Once Super Chat is enabled, whenever you run a livestream on YouTube, viewers have the ability to donate money to you through Super Chat. Any donations that you receive through Super Chat are seen under Transaction revenue. These features will unlock only after you reach 1,000 or more subscribers on your channel. So, if you are under 1,000, you won't see this stat just yet.

YouTube always takes a cut of donations you receive. For Super Chat, you receive 70 percent, and YouTube gets 30 percent. Therefore, if you receive a $10 donation, you receive $7, and YouTube gets $3.

AD RATES

Ad Rates are simply a breakdown of money you've earned through Google's display of advertisements on your videos. For every view or click of an ad per viewer, you are eligible to receive money.

WATCH TIME REPORTS

Watch time reports allow you to see who's been watching your videos, for how long, how they found your video, where they live, what devices they're using, and much more. These reports are essentially a bunch of data collected about the viewers of your video.

The watch time reports are broken up into

- Audience retention

- Demographics

- Playback locations

- Traffic sources

- Devices

- Live streaming

- Translations

The categories of demographics, playback locations, and devices are all pretty self-explanatory, but I encourage you to go through each one and see the stats for themselves!

The following sections explain the other categories in the list.

AUDIENCE RETENTION

Audience retention breaks down something called *average view duration,* which is, as the name suggests, the average time someone spent watching your video.

You really want to pay attention to this number because it tells you how long into the video a viewer watched until they stopped. If you see the average view duration for a video is 1 minute, but the actual length of the video is 2 minutes, what can you infer from that?

So what does a stat like this tell you? Why did people stop watching after 1 minute? Was there a piece of information that they needed in the video that was answered within that first minute? Was the video not what they expected, so they left? Was the video too boring or drawn-out?

These are all questions you must keep in mind when studying these analytics. Ideally, the longer average view duration, the better. A longer duration means that you kept the viewer interested, or hooked. If your videos tend to have low average view durations, what can you do in the beginning of your videos to make them want to stay longer?

REMEMBER

Try to hook the viewer in within the first few seconds and keep them interested throughout the entire video.

TRAFFIC SOURCES

Traffic sources are very interesting to me because they indicate how someone found your video. As you can see, once you're looking under Traffic sources, you can scroll down to see a list of places viewers came from that led them to your channel.

You'll more than likely see YouTube Search as one of the ways someone found your channel. That means your viewers typed something in YouTube and found your video that way. A high percentage indicates that the search terms you're including in your video, such as title, description, and tags, are working nicely. If your percentage is low, you may want to try a different approach with your titling, description, and tags.

External is another popular source other than YouTube Search that you'll see as one of your traffic sources. External simply means people found your video outside of YouTube, such as from a Facebook post, a tweet, or a Google search. If this number is higher than your YouTube search percentage, you may want to examine which source is sending people to your channel. If you click on the actual words External, 'YouTube Search, or any other traffic source listed, it will bring you to a more detailed breakdown of your traffic sources where you can analyze where they came from in greater detail.

LIVE STREAMING

Live streaming will be available only after you've live streamed on YouTube. (See Chapter 9 if you're interested in finding out more about live streaming.)

TRANSLATIONS

Just as with live streaming, Translations will display different data only if your videos have been translated into different languages.

If you're bilingual, you should consider translating your video into another language. Translating your video enables a wider audience of viewers to watch your videos.

You can apply the translation to translate a video yourself. In Chapter 6, one of the sections that is covered is how to add Subtitles/CC to your video. You apply a translation in the exact same way that you add subtitles to your video (see Chapter 6). Here's what you need to do:

1. **In the upper-right corner of your screen, click on your channel icon.**

2. **From the options that appear, click on Creator Studio.**

   You're brought to your channel's dashboard, which has many options to choose from. You can see a list of channel options on the left panel.

3. **Click on Video Manager.**

   You see all of your uploaded videos.

4. **Choose which video you'd like to add a translation to by clicking on the Edit button next to the appropriate video.**

5. **Under the video's edit options, click on the Subtitles/CC screen.**

6. **Click on Add New Subtitles/CC and type the language you'd like to translate your video into.**

7. **Then click on Create new subtitles or CC to type your own translation to go with your video.**

ENGAGEMENT REPORTS

Engagement is another word for interaction on your channel. Engagement includes likes, dislikes, comments, new subscribers, and any other way that a viewer has taken action on your channel or videos.

The Engagement reports are broken down into

- Subscribers

- Likes and dislikes

- Videos in playlists

- Comments

- Sharing

- Annotations

- Cards

- End screens

Subscribers displays data based on how many subscribers you've gained or lost. Same with Likes and dislikes — this data shows you how many likes and dislikes you've received on your channel, and you can view data on specific videos as well.

Videos in playlists gives you information based on how often your videos were added to a viewer's own playlist or favorite list. A high number here is a good thing!

Comments and sharing show data based on how often those occurred on your channel. Annotations, cards, and End screens give data based on how often viewers utilized those tools in your videos by clicking on them.

This is why it's really important to always include at least one of these in your videos! It keeps a viewer hooked on your channel and encourages them to keep watching your videos.

RESPONDING TO COMMENTS

A great way to engage with your community is to always respond to people's comments on your videos. If a viewer takes the time to comment on your video, you should always take the time to respond to them — even if it's something as simple as saying thanks!

Responding to comments shows that you're an active member of the community with an especially active channel. In addition to responding, you can also do any of the following (see Figure 8-7):

- Thumbs up a comment to like

- Thumbs down a comment you disagree with

- Select to love a comment by clicking on the heart option

Figure 8-7: You can thumbs up, thumbs down, or heart a comment.

MANAGING COMMENTS USING VISIBILITY PREFERENCES

You can also manage comments using visibility preferences:

1. **Find the video you want to respond to the comments.**

2. **Hover your mouse over the comment.**

3. **Click on the three dots that appear on the right side of the comment.**
   You see the options to

- **Pin:** Pins the current comment to the top so that your audience will see it first when scrolling through your comments.

- **Remove:** Simply deletes the comment.

- **Report spam or abuse:** If you feel the comment is inappropriate in any way, you can report it.

- **Hide user from channel:** Blocks the user from posting comments on your channel.

VIEWING YOUR COMMENTS

To view all your comments spread out between all your videos, simply head on over to your Creator Studio and follow these steps:

1. **Click on your user icon in the top-right corner and click on Creator Studio.**

2. **On the left side panel, click on Community.**

   Comments will be the first section visible. This section is where you can respond to, manage, and keep up with all the comments posted across your channel.

RESPONDING TO COMMENTS

Not all comments on your channel will be good ones. If someone leaves a bad comment, don't try to take it too personally. It happens all of the time — even the top YouTubers get flooded with thousands of comments a day, and not all of them are nice.

Fortunately, YouTube can automatically filter out inappropriate language so that you can approve of comments that are flagged. Here's how you can protect your account from bad language and spam:

1. **Sign in to your YouTube account and go to your Creator Studio.**

2. **Click on Community and go to Community settings.**

3. **Look for Default settings toward the bottom.**

4. **Click on Hold potentially inappropriate comments for review (see Figure 8-8).**

Now any potentially inappropriate or spam messages will be held for review.

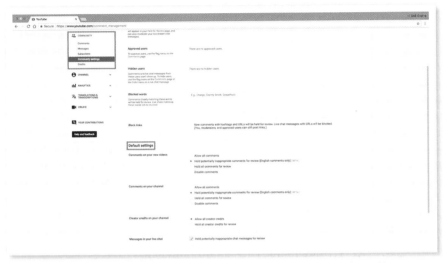

Figure 8-8: Find the default settings under Community to update your privacy settings with comments.

APPROVING OR DISCARDING COMMENTS

To approve or discard these comments:

1. **While still under Community, click on Comments.**

2. **Click on Held for review and Likely spam (see Figure 8-9).**

   If there are any comments held for review or spam, they will be listed here. You can now choose to approve these comments, delete them, or report them for spam or abuse.

Figure 8-9: View comments that have been held for review.

You can download the YouTube Studio app on your mobile device to check on your channel, respond to comments, and much more!

EXPLORING FURTHER

I encourage you to explore YouTube analytics on your own by clicking through each category under Analytics. Try different videos and different time spans and check out specific reports.

Here's a cool way to view your channel's growth by subscribers each month:

1. **Under Analytics, click on Subscribers.**

   You see an overview of your subscriber growth.

2. **In the upper-left corner, select your date range.**

   To view your channel's growth over the last year, click on Last 365 Days (see Figure 8-10).

3. **From the same screen, click on Monthly from the menu, which is also shown in Figure 8-10.**

4. **Hover your mouse over different areas of the line chart to view how many subscribers you've gained each month for the past year.**

Figure 8-10: Your Subscribers overview under your channel's Analytics.

09

Going Further with More Features

After you establish your channel and feel comfortable with everything you've set up, you can work on more features that unlock over time as your channel gains more popularity. These features include live streaming and monetization, which is a fancy word for a way to earn money through ads played on your videos.

MAKING MONEY WITH YOUR VIDEOS

REMEMBER

It's really important to understand that you need to prioritize getting more views and subscribers over making money. If you create a YouTube channel with the single goal of earning money, you're going to be disappointed.

You can make money from your YouTube videos. As a forewarning, you aren't going to make a lot of money right away. In fact, it may take you months, or even a year, to get your first paycheck from YouTube. But with dedication and hard work, your channel will grow over time and eventually be able to earn money.

More subscribers means more views, and more views means you can earn more money from your monetized videos. But without views, you won't even have an opportunity to make money.

SIGNING UP FOR YOUTUBE'S PARTNER PROGRAM

After you get 10,000 views on your channel, you become eligible for YouTube's Partner Program. By signing up with YouTube's Partner Program, you'll then be able to start earning money through your YouTube Channel.

The reason YouTube set a 10,000-view threshold is to be able to check the validity of a channel. Many fake scam accounts exist on YouTube that simply take another creator's content and repost it to make a quick buck. By having a 10,000-view requirement, YouTube can ensure that your channel is legit.

Start by figuring out how many total views are on your channel:

1. **Log into your YouTube account.**

2. **Head on over to your Creator Studio and make sure that your Dashboard is selected (see Figure 9-1).**

   Your views and subscribers appear, as shown in Figure 9-2.

   Below 10,000 views? That's okay — you'll get there! Continue to upload consistently and be patient. Learn from your analytics and keep finding creative ways to get more subs and viewers!

   Over 10,000 views? Awesome! Continue with the following steps.

3. **If you're over 10,000 views, make sure that you're logged into your account and go to** www.youtube.com/account_monetization **(see Figure 9-3).**

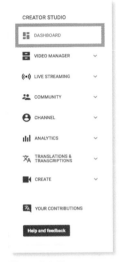

Figure 9-1: The Dashboard section of your channel's Creator Studio.

Figure 9-2: Your channel's total views and subscribers.

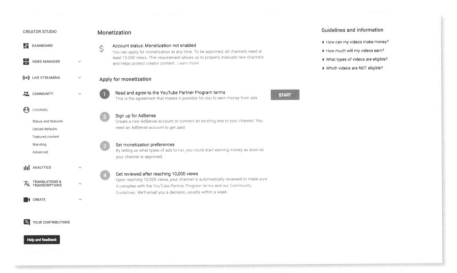

Figure 9-3: The page to get you started with YouTube's monetization.

4. **Read and agree to the YouTube Partner Program terms.**

   This is the first step that covers all policies and legal aspects of making money on YouTube. It's important to read and only agree after you've gone through it. Don't be afraid to ask a family member or friend to help reading through the guidelines if it's too much for you.

5. **Sign up for Google AdSense.**

   You need to create an AdSense account (see Figure 9-4) to view your earning status and actually get paid. It's free to set up an AdSense account.

Figure 9-4: YouTube's AdSense account creation page.

6. **Set your preferences.**

   In this section, you can choose how you want ads to be displayed on your videos. You can always go back and change these preferences later.

7. **Give it time.**

   You may not get approved right away, so don't worry if you have to wait a few days or even weeks before your channel gets approved for monetization after reaching 10,000 views. There are many applications, and YouTube must go through each account to make sure that they aren't fake.

SETTING GOALS FOR YOURSELF

The key to earning money on your videos is your audience. Advertisers want channels that have lots of traffic so that their ads gain the most exposure. If you were trying to advertise a product, wouldn't you want your ad somewhere it could gain a lot of views?

I would recommend starting with very simple goals when it comes to making money on YouTube. By studying your Analytics (see Chapter 8), your revenue reports will give you lots of insight on how much money you're earning through your videos. Start small with a goal of earning $1. Although it sounds very small, you'll be surprised how many views it takes to earn $1 on YouTube.

Generally from my experience, 1,000 views on smaller channels roughly equates to $1, while 10,000 views is about $10. This ballpark estimate isn't exact, and sometimes you'll earn more or less depending on the length of the video and your audience.

After you earn the first dollar, aim higher. See which of your videos are most popular by checking out your YouTube analytics. If you've got 20 videos, which are the top 5 in terms of views and earnings? Why were these videos successful? What made them stand out?

Play into holidays and certain events throughout the year. Is Halloween close by? Why not make a Halloween-themed video? Summer break from school approaching? Think of summer-themed videos you can create to stay current.

LIVE STREAMING ON YOUTUBE

Live streaming is the act of broadcasting something live, over the Internet, in real time as it's happening. As live streaming has become more mainstream, many social media apps, such as Facebook, Instagram, and Twitter, have adapted to create their own live stream capability.

Over the past several years, live streaming has grown immensely in popularity, especially in gaming communities with sites such as Twitch.tv and Mixer. YouTube has also joined the party by releasing YouTube Live, where creators can now live stream from their very own channels. On YouTube Live, users stream games, live music, Q&A with viewers, the latest news, and more.

Live streaming on YouTube Live is a great way to connect with your subscribers in real-time. It's also awesome for your channel to gain more exposure. Live streaming is raw and unscripted, and little production is needed. You can livestream from your computer or mobile device all while interacting with viewers in your chat.

Unlike filming and editing a video, with live streaming, there is no work after you go offline. Your live stream is automatically uploaded to your channel just like one of your videos and is eligible for monetization as long as you don't break any copyright rules, such as playing non-original music in the background.

SETTING UP YOUR LIVE STREAM

Just like with monetizing, to set up live streaming, you need to go through a verification process with YouTube. That way, YouTube can make sure that your account is in good standing. To set up your live stream:

1. **Head over to your Creator Studio.**

2. **Select Live Streaming on the left side panel, as shown in Figure 9-5.**

3. **Click on Get Started (see Figure 9-6).**

4. **Go through the account verification process.**

   After you're approved, you can begin your first live stream!

Figure 9-5: The live streaming section of your channel's Creator Studio.

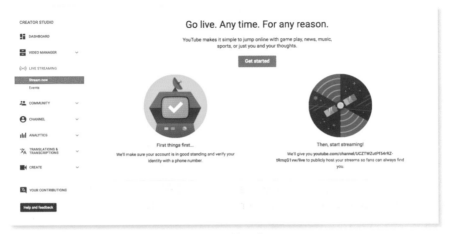

Figure 9-6: The screen you see the first time you decide to live stream.

Unless you have violations on your account, there should be no reason for you to not get approved for live streaming. If you don't get approved right away, just be patient. YouTube has millions of accounts to scan through.

ON MOBILE

Live streaming can be really fun and exciting, but takes a little bit of prep work to get started. You can stream instantly through a mobile device on the YouTube app, which you can download for free.

After you download the YouTube app:

1. **Open your YouTube app and select the video camera icon by the top of your screen (see Figure 9-7).**

   Figures 9-7, 9-8, and 9-9 are screenshots from the iPhone YouTube app. Icons may be different depending on your phone, but should be very similar.

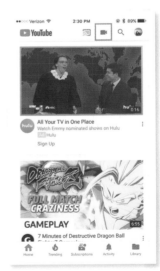

Figure 9-7: The icon to go live on the iPhone's YouTube app.

2. **Click on Go Live (see Figure 9-8).**

3. **Select a Title, Privacy, and any additional settings with the gear icon (see Figure 9-9).**

   You're ready to go live!

Figure 9-8: Tap on Go Live to begin your mobile live stream.

Figure 9-9: The screen to type in your title and set other options.

ON A COMPUTER

If you have a webcam on your computer, you can live stream. But, you will also need to download an additional piece of software called an *encoder*.

An encoder is a fancy word for a program that captures content from your computer — games, audio, video, and much more — and allows the content to be sent to YouTube to stream. An encoder is essentially an in-between program for you and YouTube — for example, Your Content⇨Encoding Software⇨YouTube.

So what's the best encoder to use? YouTube Live has its own list of verified streaming software, shown in Figure 9-10.

Figure 9-10: A listing of YouTube's recommended streaming encoders.

The choice of which encoder to use is yours alone. If you're going mostly mobile, definitely use the YouTube app on your smartphone. As for game capture on a console like Xbox, PlayStation, or Wii U, Elgato Game Capture has been around for years and is a dependable source. For Mac or PC gaming, I personally use OBS or — Open Broadcaster Software, but many people also use XSplit, too!

To choose an encoder, ask yourself these questions:

- Are you doing mostly mobile, on-the-go streams?

- Are you capturing content from a gaming console?

- Are you live streaming from a computer?

Narrow it down from there, explore your options, and see what works best for you!

The same rules apply to your videos. Remember to abide by YouTube's terms and conditions while live streaming.

SETTING UP YOUR ENCODER

Because I use OBS, I am going to use it in this section to demonstrate how I set it up for live streaming. You must go through a few basic steps in order to successfully go live. These steps are similar no matter which program you use.

The information you need to go live will be under your Broadcast Settings tab (see Figure 9-11). In my case, I have the following settings selected in my OBS software:

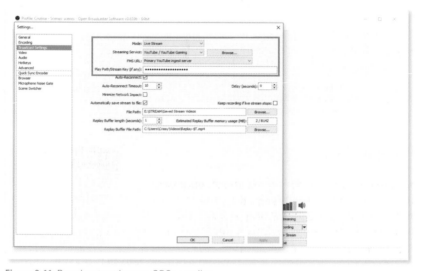

Figure 9-11: Broadcast settings on OBS to go live.

- **Mode:**   Live Stream

- **Streaming service:**   YouTube/YouTube Gaming

- **FMS URL:**   Primary YouTube ingest server

- **Play path/stream key:**   Vital to going live —find the key on your YouTube live page, shown in Figure 9-12

You can find your key on your YouTube live page. Under your Live Streaming tab in Creator Studio, scroll all the way to the bottom to find your Encoder Settings. This key won't be visible until after you're approved for live streaming.

ENCODER SETUP

Server URL

rtmp://a.rtmp.youtube.com/live2

Stream name/key

•••••••••••••••••••   Reveal

Figure 9-12: You must copy and paste your stream key, found here, into the OBS Broadcast Settings.

Your stream key is just as secret as a password, so never share it with anyone else! Keep it private. If someone else gets hold of your stream key, they can go live on your channel. This is why your stream key is encrypted to look like a password.

PLANNING A LIVE STREAM

Just like creating a video, think about what you want to do in your live stream. If you're playing a game, what will you be doing in game? Is it going to be entertaining? If you're doing an IRL, mobile stream, have a plan! Where are you going?

REMEMBER

Be sure to apply your changes. Mode, streaming service, and stream key are three vital settings you need to set up before you can go live. Without specifying those three settings, you can't live stream.

IRL stands for in real life, and many popular streamers do outside/IRL streams now. IRL gives viewers a look at a day in the life of their favorite YouTuber.

Here are a few more tips for planning your live stream:

- **Stay connected with your chat.**   Make sure your chat is visible, no matter what platform you're using to live stream. Interacting with your chat keeps your viewers engaged and more likely to stay. Saying hi to your chatters, welcoming and thanking them, and asking questions are all ways to keep them active!

- **The longer you live stream, the better.**   Your subscribers get notified when you go live, but they won't always tune in right away. The longer your livestream is, the better chance you have to get recognized by subscribers as well as new viewers.

- **Spread the word!**   You can schedule a live stream under Live Streaming⇨Events in your Creator Studio so that viewers can expect your next stream. You can also tell your friends and blast it out on your social media to get the word out there.

- **See what others are doing.**   Check out http://gaming.youtube.com (see Figure 9-13) to check out other YouTubers' live streams. See how they have their interface set up. How do they interact with their chat? How do they make their live streams entertaining? Why would you want to watch your own live stream?

Figure 9-13: YouTube Gaming's homepage.

CHECKING THE STATS!

After you end your live stream, it automatically gets uploaded to your Video Manager. You can tell the difference between a live stream and a regular video upload because under your title, it will say either Streamed or Published. (see Figure 9-14)

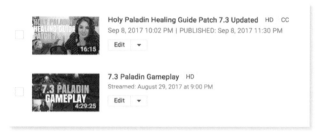

Figure 9-14: The video on top says it was published, while the video underneath says it was streamed.

Just like with your videos, you can view stats on your live streams. It takes one to three days for YouTube to process the stats for your live stream. If you just ended your steam, you won't be able to view specific stats for a couple of days. After the data is ready, you can check your stats:

1. **Click on Analytics on the left side of your Creator Studio.**

2. **Under Watch time reports, select Live streaming.**

3. **Select which specific live stream you want to focus on.**

    You can see how many viewers saw your livestream and how many chat messages were sent! (Refer to Figure 9-15).

Figure 9-15: A nifty graph designed to show your viewer stats.

In most of my streams, the viewer count slowly goes up as time goes on and then drops down toward the end of the stream. Don't be discouraged if you don't have a lot of viewers right away.

ENABLING SPONSORSHIPS

Sponsorships is one of the newest features to come from YouTube Live. For $4.99 a month, users can pay to sponsor your channel to get a custom icon next to their name in your live chat as well as custom icons and emojis. These perks are only available to those who sponsor your channel. Sponsorships are essentially a new way for creators like yourself to make more money on YouTube.

As you gain more sponsors, you'll be able to unlock new features, such as more custom emojis and perks for your viewers. However, you must meet certain requirements before you can enable sponsorships.

To be eligible for sponsorships on YouTube Gaming, you must meet these requirements:

- You've got a Gaming channel.

- Live streaming is set up on your channel.

- You have a Google AdSense account for monetization.

- Your channel has over 1,000 subscribers.

- You are over 18 years old.

- You are located in one of the available locations.

- You follow YouTube's terms and policies.

As of its launch. sponsorships are eligible only for gaming channels. However, YouTube eventually plans to unlock this feature for all channels, not just gamers! So, by the time you read this section, sponsorships may already be open to all creators on YouTube who meet the preceding requirements.

To enable sponsorships:

1. **Log into your YouTube account.**

2. **Go to your Features page at** www.youtube.com/features.

3. **Scan through your features until you find Sponsorships, select Enable, and follow the on-screen instructions.**

After you have your sponsorships enabled, users will see the sponsor icon appear in your channel under YouTube live.

Figure 9-16: The green Sponsor button means you can start getting your own sponsors.

A green Sponsor button will appear under your live stream video after you've enabled and been approved for sponsorships (see Figure 9-16). This button will not appear under regularly uploaded videos, just live streams.

ORGANIZING PLAYLISTS

After you upload or live stream videos to your account, you'll want to stay on top of everything to keep it nice and organized. Each playlist should have a specific theme, such as Food Reviews for all food-related videos or New Game Reviews for game reviews.

CREATING A PLAYLIST

To make a new playlist:

1. **Go to your Creator Studio.**

2. **Select Video Manager.**
   Several options pop up underneath your Video Manager.

3. **Click on Playlists, as shown in Figure 9-17.**

4. **On the upper-left side, click on New Playlist (see Figure 9-18).**

Figure 9-17: The Playlists section under your channel's Video Manager.

Figure 9-18: Create your playlist.

5. **Name your playlist and set its privacy.**

6. **Click on Create after you're finished.**

After you create a playlist, click on Edit and then Add Videos to add videos to your playlist.

DISPLAYING PLAYLISTS ON YOUR CHANNEL'S MAIN PAGE

A great way to keep your channel organized is to add all your videos to playlists to display on your channel's main page. Here's how:

1. **Log in to your YouTube Channel.**

2. **Click on Edit Layout.**

3. **Scroll to the bottom and click on Add a section (see Figure 9-19).**

4. **Select which content you'd like to add.**

5. **To add a single playlist to your channel, click on Single Playlist (see Figure 9-20).**

6. **Select Horizontal Row.**

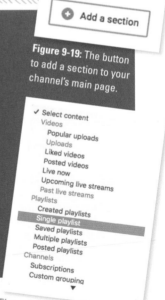

Figure 9-19: The button to add a section to your channel's main page.

Figure 9-20: The option to add a Single playlist to your channel's main page.

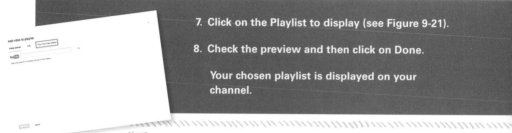

7. Click on the Playlist to display (see Figure 9-21).

8. Check the preview and then click on Done.

   Your chosen playlist is displayed on your channel.

Figure 9-21: By clicking on Your YouTube videos, you can choose videos directly from your own channel to be added to your playlist.

You can display playlists differently on your channel. Play around with the Playlist settings to see what you like best!

NOTES

NOTES

NOTES

NOTES

CRISTINA CALABRESE has been an active member of the YouTube community for more than ten years, using her experience as the driving force behind her writing. She currently works as the Director of Marketing & Communications for The Digital Arts Experience, a STEAM-focused tech education startup for kids. Cristina works with YouTube, video-making, content strategy, and digital marketing analysis on a daily basis.

DEDICATION

I'd like to dedicate this book to my parents, Nicholas and Loretta Calabrese, and my sister, Dr. Victoria Calabrese, who have always supported my crazy endeavors and encouraged me to turn my creative ideas into realities. Thank you for being my No. 1 fans.

AUTHOR'S ACKNOWLEDGMENTS

I would not have been given the opportunity to work on this project had it not been for Rob Kissner and The Digital Arts Experience (The DAE). Rob, thank you for believing in me and trusting that I will always put in 100 percent effort. Thank you for being such a positive force in my life and always finding ways to make me laugh.

I'm grateful to the entire team at The DAE who make coming to work an absolute pleasure. Emily Angell, thank you for involving me in the production of your music videos over the years, where I learned so much about filming, video editing, keywording, and analytics. To Big Nick, the ultimate dungeon master, and Lory, a brilliant designer. Patrick, thank you for the constant book updates and random *Star Wars* facts.

Thank you to Steve Hayes and the team at Wiley, including Kelly Ewing, for the guidance through this whole process. A special thank you to Matt Kissner for the constant support throughout the years.

PUBLISHER'S ACKNOWLEDGMENTS

SENIOR ACQUISITIONS EDITOR: Steve Hayes

PROJECT EDITOR: Kelly Ewing

COPY EDITOR: Kelly Ewing

SR. EDITORIAL ASSISTANT: Cherie Case

PRODUCTION EDITOR: Tamilmani Varadharaj

COVER IMAGE: © FrankRamspott / iStockphoto

Leverage the powe

Dummies is the global leader in the reference category and one of the most trusted and highly regarded brands in the world. No longer just focused on books, customers now have access to the dummies content they need in the format they want. Together we'll craft a solution that engages your customers, stands out from the competition, and helps you meet your goals.

Advertising & Sponsorships

Connect with an engaged audience on a powerful multimedia site, and position your message alongside expert how-to content. Dummies.com is a one-stop shop for free, online information and know-how curated by a team of experts.

- Targeted ads
- Video
- Email Marketing
- Microsites
- Sweepstakes sponsorship

20 MILLION PAGE VIEWS EVERY SINGLE MONTH

15 MILLION UNIQUE VISITORS PER MONTH

43% OF ALL VISITORS ACCESS THE SITE VIA THEIR MOBILE DEVICES

700,000 NEWSLET SUBSCRIPTI TO THE INBOXES OF
300,000 UNIQUE INDIVIDUALS EVERY WEEK

# of dummies

Custom Publishing

Reach a global audience in any language by creating a solution that will differentiate you from competitors, amplify your message, and encourage customers to make a buying decision.

- Apps
- Books
- eBooks
- Video
- Audio
- Webinars

Brand Licensing & Content

Leverage the strength of the world's most popular reference brand to reach new audiences and channels of distribution.

For more information, visit **dummies.com/biz**

PERSONAL ENRICHMENT

9781119187790	9781119179030	9781119293354	9781119293347	9781119310068	9781119235606
USA $26.00	USA $21.99	USA $24.99	USA $22.99	USA $22.99	USA $24.99
CAN $31.99	CAN $25.99	CAN $29.99	CAN $27.99	CAN $27.99	CAN $29.99
UK £19.99	UK £16.99	UK £17.99	UK £16.99	UK £16.99	UK £17.99

9781119251163	9781119235491	9781119279952	9781119283133	9781119287117	9781119130246
USA $24.99	USA $26.99	USA $24.99	USA $24.99	USA $24.99	USA $22.99
CAN $29.99	CAN $31.99	CAN $29.99	CAN $29.99	CAN $29.99	CAN $27.99
UK £17.99	UK £19.99	UK £17.99	UK £17.99	UK £16.99	UK £16.99

PROFESSIONAL DEVELOPMENT

9781119311041	9781119255796	9781119293439	9781119281467	9781119280651	9781119251132	9781119310
USA $24.99	USA $39.99	USA $26.99	USA $26.99	USA $29.99	USA $24.99	USA $34.00
CAN $29.99	CAN $47.99	CAN $31.99	CAN $31.99	CAN $35.99	CAN $29.99	CAN $41.99
UK £17.99	UK £27.99	UK £19.99	UK £19.99	UK £21.99	UK £17.99	UK £24.99

9781119181705	9781119263593	9781119257769	9781119293477	9781119265313	9781119239314	9781119293
USA $29.99	USA $26.99	USA $29.99	USA $26.99	USA $24.99	USA $29.99	USA $35.99
CAN $35.99	CAN $31.99	CAN $35.99	CAN $31.99	CAN $29.99	CAN $35.99	CAN $35.99
UK £21.99	UK £19.99	UK £21.99	UK £19.99	UK £17.99	UK £21.99	UK £21.99

dummies
A Wiley Bran

Learning Made Easy

ACADEMIC

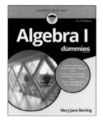

9781119293576
USA $19.99
CAN $23.99
UK £15.99

9781119293637
USA $19.99
CAN $23.99
UK £15.99

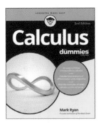

9781119293491
USA $19.99
CAN $23.99
UK £15.99

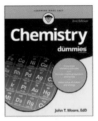

9781119293460
USA $19.99
CAN $23.99
UK £15.99

9781119293590
USA $19.99
CAN $23.99
UK £15.99

9781119215844
USA $26.99
CAN $31.99
UK £19.99

9781119293378
USA $22.99
CAN $27.99
UK £16.99

9781119293521
USA $19.99
CAN $23.99
UK £15.99

9781119239178
USA $18.99
CAN $22.99
UK £14.99

9781119263883
USA $26.99
CAN $31.99
UK £19.99

Available Everywhere Books Are Sold

dummies.com

Small books for big imaginations

GETTING STARTED WITH **Coding**
Get Creative with Code!
Camille McCue, PhD

9781119177173
USA $9.99
CAN $9.99
UK £8.99

MODDING **Minecraft**
Build Your Own Minecraft Mods!
Sarah Guthals, PhD
Stephen Foster, PhD
Lindsey Handley, PhD

9781119177272
USA $9.99
CAN $9.99
UK £8.99

MAKING **YouTube** VIDEOS
Star in Your Own Video!
Nick Willoughby

9781119177241
USA $9.99
CAN $9.99
UK £8.99

DESIGNING **Digital Games**
Create Games with Scratch!
Derek Breen

9781119177210
USA $9.99
CAN $9.99
UK £8.99

GETTING STARTED WITH **Raspberry Pi**
Program Your Raspberry Pi!
Richard Wentk

9781119262657
USA $9.99
CAN $9.99
UK £6.99

EXPERIMENTING WITH **Science**
Think, Test, and Learn!
Olivia J. Mullins, PhD

9781119291336
USA $9.99
CAN $9.99
UK £6.99

CREATING **Digital Animations**
Animate Stories with Scratch!
Derek Breen

9781119233527
USA $9.99
CAN $9.99
UK £6.99

GETTING STARTED WITH **Engineering**
Think Like an Engineer!
Camille McCue, PhD

9781119291220
USA $9.99
CAN $9.99
UK £6.99

WRITING **Computer Code**
Learn the Language of Computers!
Chris Minnick and Eva Holland

9781119177302
USA $9.99
CAN $9.99
UK £8.99

Unleash Their Creativity

dummies.com

dummies
A Wiley Brand